The Sicilian Experience of

Mr. Benny

❖

*The Five-Generation Saga
of a Sicilian American Family*

JB ZITO

Order this book online at www.trafford.com
or email orders@trafford.com

Most Trafford titles are also available at major online book retailers.

Printed in the United States of America.

ISBN: 978-1-4669-2945-6 (sc)
ISBN: 978-1-4669-2944-9 (hc)
ISBN: 978-1-4669-2946-3 (e)

Library of Congress Control Number: 2012906931

Trafford rev. 04/24/2012

 www.trafford.com

North America & international
toll-free: 1 888 232 4444 (USA & Canada)
phone: 250 383 6864 • fax: 812 355 4082

This book is dedicated to the entire Zito family and all of the families joined with us in this life. I especially want to recognize my sons, Thomas Benjamin, and Jack Edward.

CONTENTS

FATHER-FATHER-FATHER

(PART I OF III)

SALVATORE 1888

THE BOY CARRIED less sulfur than usual this time. His muscles were twitching. The mine was nearly a hundred meters deep. The twists and turns of the cavern, descending through never ending sulfur walls, down, and then back to the surface, created a throbbing in his back and legs. His mind fought this pain, but he was too tired. The brief intermittent exchange of glorious blue sky, gave him some sense of hope to keep on living. The process was repeated, again and again, until his emotions were dulled to the point where he felt nothing but a muted existence, a spinning painter's palette of dull yellow and white.

Four years ago, his reactions were acute. Now, those same oscillations of light and darkness, of despair and hope, changed to a bland acceptance of what was real. Repeat visits to the Devils' gates, through purgatory and back to the surface of the earth, gave him a feeling that this was a life and death experience, not unlike that of Christ carrying his cross to Golgotha, "The Place of the Skulls." However, Salvatore did not die on any of these days. Over a hundred round trips, each day, had not taken his life from him.

Naked, with only a loincloth, sweat poured from his body. While in the deepest recesses of the abyss, he caught a cramp that forced him to put his bag of ore down. He had to rest on his back, and curl his toes towards the roof of the cave to stretch his calf muscle until it stopped its contraction. This caused him to lose some time on this round. It would cost him more than a cramp.

The foreman was waiting impatiently for him to return with his bag of sulfur. Adolfo was perturbed that Salvatore was slow, and carrying a load with much less volume than customary. He whacked the boy-slave with a stick across his buttocks. The yellow dust flew from him after the strike. He dropped to his knees and gasped.

The next time it will be the whip!

Sal understood quickly and did not wish to feel that whip.

His hatred for Adolfo overwhelmed his being. The emotion surged forward from the depths of his soul. Raw bile frothed into his mouth. This bitter taste he knew too often. He knew he must not fight back against Adolfo. Cruelty was the natural order of the day for this sulfur mine.

Reason overruled anger. Salvatore would not raise his eyes toward his tormentor, for this would only bring on more punishment. He had been through this many times before. He dumped the bag into the ore cart, and descended again to the depths of the mine. The shaft was narrow and serpentine. Even the shorter boys had to squat low and eventually, this constant stooped position, created back problems for every child that worked in the mines.

His memory could help to soothe his anger. He remembered a time when he was sent to the mines, to repay the "debt" that his family owed the Mafia. He could recall the time when the family were all at the Cape of San Vito lo Capo. The water was crystalline clear and the beach extended forever until it reached the mountain rising from the sea. He and his sister were naked, running in the surf as it cascaded upon the white beach. After bathing, his mother threw a towel around him and hugged him to her bare breasts. He could smell the sweetness of her and the olive oil she had rubbed on their bodies. His father gave them, fruit, freshly picked, and when he bit into the orange, the sugary liquid ran across his lips and dripped upon his chest. They dived back into the sea to wash off, and the day was as real to him as yesterday. His parents drank wine from a bottle they shared and smiled at him and his sister building castles of sand. The picnic basket was full of fruit, nuts, and bread.

This was his remembrance of the good life, before the land keepers died and the new owners arrived. Then it seemed they could not grow enough fruit, or make enough wine to satisfy the owners. They could not gather enough eggs from the chickens, nor milk enough from the goats. These new men wanted more and more, and he remembered the frustration on his parents faces.

It was then that he was taken from his family at eight years of age to work to pay the family debt. His parents were told that he would return after the debt was paid, but no amount of toil could ever repay the amount of money needed. So now, this was his existence. He was told that his family had escaped to one of the Americas. He did not know of these places, or how he would ever find them. Why they did not come and rescue him was a wonder. He had long given up that hope of reunion to the reality of this slavery.

Often, the young men collided with one another because much of the time, their vision was very poor. Sulfur dust, in and around their eyes created a nagging, burning sensation. Secondly, from their posture, they saw only their own feet and legs. The echoing sounds of shuffling feet were constant, and the carriers never knew if it was of their own creation, or someone coming the other way. After hours of tortuous toiling, he was stumbling and sweating once more towards the depths of Hell, when he collided with a child miner traveling in the opposite direction. Both of them fell to the dirt floor of the shaft. Salvatore immediately offered an apology.

I am so sorry boy. I wasn't watching where—
I am not a boy!
What?
Salvatore was stunned.

I am a girl!

You are a girl? Here?—In this mine? How long?

She didn't respond, but rather, scrambled to her feet and kept climbing upward with her sack of dust.

Salvatore was silent and stared after her until she rounded the bend. He could barely see by the lantern light. He began to square his mind.

Questi animali stopped at nothing, even to enslave young girls.

Salvatore knew his life was relegated to slavery, being sold by his parents to the *famiglia*. However, he had no idea someone would give their little girl away to life of hard labor.

On the way up with the next load she nudged him gently, traveling in the opposite direction.

When she was about three steps past him, she shouted over her shoulder.

Nove giorni!—nome e Marianna!

No wonder she was so strong. She has only been here a nine days. Soon she will break down.

The children, along with the few men that worked, ate dinner together. The meals were sparse and it was a "camp-style" setting. Every day after their collision, Salvatore sat next to Mariana. They became best of friends, and whispered to each other on every occasion possible. On Sunday mornings, they would have a break for Mass with Father Dominic from the cathedral of St. Giuseppe. He would travel to the church near the mine on Sundays. He did this for the children. Father invited them both to the rectory after mass. He secreted instructions during confession. This became a regular happening for the three of them. Father Dominic would bring some small amount of food with him hidden in his robes. These two young children, he came to love and pity. The bread and sausage he was able to give them, became life sustaining.

Father came to know all about them, asking their age, and inquiring about their *famiglia*. To him, it could not be possible that

God had granted these two beautiful children, a life of slavery in these mines.

What good could come of all of this insanity?

He did have some power and maybe, somehow, he could intervene on behalf of Marianna and Salvatore. The priests fell into a category of caretakers of souls, between the powerful families and the peasants. They commanded a modicum of respect, even from the most powerful **_Dons_**.

Salvatore and Maria went to the rectory and met with Father Dominic. There was some laughing coming from the room. The good priest was trying to raise some hope for these children. He constantly spoke with them about the trials Christ faced in his life, and how these children should look to Him for reassurance in times of despair.

Adolfo watched from behind a church column.

These two should not have more privileges than the other children.

He would continue to spy on Sunday mornings. Then one Sunday morning, he slipped into the rectory and confronted all three of them together. Father Dominic quickly covered stating that he was giving the rite of confirmation to the children.

I am only helping them to learn their prayers properly.

This day went by without incident. Adolfo was not convinced of Father Dominic's sincerity. Adolfo did not believe in the priests or any of the church doctrine. All that mattered was that he was the gate keeper to hell. He relied upon fear. As all of those with power, he used fear as his major weapon. He hated those children most, who did not respect his authority. When the children showed no fear of his whip, he would burn them with a lantern the next time. He would scald their calves to make them remember him.

Pain and fear—Fear and pain—this is what these children know! I am the one who has the power and authority here! I can even create a living Hell if I wish.

Half way through the week, Adolfo confronted Marianna when she returned to the top of the mine shaft. She lied about the situation in the church to protect Salvatore, Father Dominic, and herself, as well. Adolfo told her to turn around, and he whipped her viciously across her calves twice. He then forced her to drop the top of her robe, a meager cloth, and whipped her across her back, sending blood seeping through her garment and down her back. He warned her not to be seen with Salvatore again at the church. They must sit apart, both there and at meals. Marianna did not cry but turned to face her tormentor, covering her small breasts with her hands. Adolfo laughed at her modesty and made derogatory comments. She was used to this kind of ridicule from him. He made these comments to enhance his own ego. His own anger was cast upon those less fortunate.

He commanded her to hurry back to work. She ran back down the shaft, pulling her ore bag behind her. Halfway down, under the dim lantern light, she found Salvatore and stumbled into him, out of breath. She embraced him with all of her strength that was left. Salvatore was surprised and dropped his bag of sulfur. He hugged her cautiously, not knowing what was happening. At first, he thought it was Marianna's sweat that soaked through her robe. Then, in the shadowy corridor, he could discern the darkness of blood, and his hands were covered, dripping, with the precious fluids oozing forth. He asked her.

What is this Marianna?

Quel bastardo ha battuto su di me. (That bastard beat on me.)

It took a moment for the whole incident to register with Salvatore. He was exhausted, but he knew he must retaliate against the hated man. Marianna begged him not to, for he might be killed. She knew Adolfo was looking for an excuse to do exactly that. Salvatore thought about what he must do. Then he told Marianna not to do anything. Just go about business as usual. Each time they passed, Salvatore related a little more to her about his plan. Essentially, he kept saying to her—

Please—just make it to Mass on Sunday. Act like you are not affected by all of this. Everything as usual. Stay calm.

Every time he dropped his ore into the cart, he could feel Adolfo's eyes piercing him. He was careful not to make eye contact or do anything out of the ordinary, physically, or emotionally. It was difficult to reign in his emotions. He would do what was necessary.

At every meal, Salvatore sat as far from her as possible. He did not wish to give away his plan.

Adolfo was pleased that he had exerted and imposed his power over these children.

Adolfo did not know Salvatore's strength. Four years of hauling sulfur will either kill you or make you powerful. You will either become a person of despair, or one of hope. Salvatore had a strong disposition and did not allow himself the luxury of self-pity. Salvatore had no true hope for a good life until he met Marianna and Father Dominic. These were the only people he knew now. His parents had long been forgotten. Being sold into slavery had severed his relationship. Sal was alone in this world. Now he had others to watch out for. Marianna made him larger than himself. She and Father Dominic were the only people he knew that he cared about. Sal thought to himself often about religion.

If there is a Jesus, where is he? If he is to save the world, why am I punished this way? Why is a person like Adolfo allowed to live?

Sunday morning brought on the usual routine. It was a short walk to the Chapel. He was not surprised that Marianna's wrap was still covered with dark stains. Few noticed because all of the children had some semblance of grime, sweat, and dried blood upon them. To her surprise, Sam sat in the pew next to her, and nervously, she slid a few feet away. Sam sidled close to her again. She asked-.

Cosa stai facendo? (What are you doing?)

Sal whispered not to worry. She glanced over her shoulder and Adolfo was watching them. Her body cringed in fear for what was going to happen to them. When mass was ended, and church hall was empty, Sal grabbed her by the elbow and guided her towards the rectory. Father Dominic would be there. When they arrived, Sal looked quickly through the crack in the door and noticed Adolfo moving slowly towards them. Salvatore acted as though nothing was wrong but Marianna was already pleading with Father Dominic to help them.

When Adolfo barged through the door, Father Dominic rose to defend Marianna. Adolfo pushed the priest hard and the elderly man fell to the floor. Adolfo put his hands around Marianna's neck. At that moment, the small stone statuette of St. Mary descended from the sky and fell on the back of Adolfo's head. He rolled over dazed. Sal quickly grabbed his pistol from his shoulder holster. He gave it to Father Dominic who was struggling to stand. Then Sal was upon the body of Adolfo. He let out all of his anger, punching him in the face, as hard as he could, over and over and over, until Marianna and the priest could pull him off. Blood was gushing from Adolfo's nose and mouth. Father Dominic was worried that Adolfo might be dead, but then began thinking about what he must do next. He looked out into the church. No one was there who saw what happened.

Once Adolfo started to recover, Father Dominic had Sal tie Adolfo's arms and legs and they put him in the back of the priest's wagon. Immediately, the four of them began a journey. It was high noon.

THE DEAL

T HE DONKEY HELD a slow and steady pace across the barren interior of Sicily. The yellow and brown rocky ground reflected the sun's rays back into the sweltering atmosphere. Many places in Sicily were like a Garden of Eden, but this place was a bleak and corrosive as the Devil's front yard. It was like a cauldron of dust and air mixture that was on fire.

Father handed Adolfo over to the guards and told them to look after him until he had a chance to speak with Don Rimado. Walking inside the office, the difference in heat and light made the good Father adjust his sight by covering and rubbing his eyes for a moment.

The Don greeted him with the usual respectful greeting for a man of the cloth. He could immediately see the serious look on Father Dominic's face, and then Marianna and Salvatore were ushered in by two of the guards. Don Rimado spoke with authority.

Leave them to me. Please go! Andare ora!

Father Dominic explained everything just as it happened. Then Don Rimado asked Sal and Marianna about their recollection of the incident. He asked a few more questions regarding provocation by Adolfo.

Why did this man hit you? What did you do to make him so angry? Did you try to strike him first? Did he provide you with enough water to drink? Where you working as fast as you could carry?

Salvatore and Marianna were more confused than anything as to why this foreman would be so angry with them. They were working hard.

The Don said he would do what he could and he released the two to Father Dominic's care. The Don thought it best that they all return to the church headquarters in Palermo until he could settle on what to do.

The priest was very happy with this humane and sensible decision and quickly left with Marianna and Salvatore in the wagon.

The guards glared at them as they left, while Adolfo lay in a back storage room. He knew a meeting with Don Rimado was coming and it would not be a good one. His fear of Don Rimado was real. Even having this fear, he showed little respect for Don Rimado's orders. He was constantly being reminded that the use of too much force did not help the production in the mine. The pickaxe men (*piconieri*) needed their carriers (*carusi*) to stay as strong and healthy as possible to manage the loads more quickly. Constantly beating the children served no purpose other than to create animosity towards everyone at the mine. Public opinion was creating havoc with the local government supporting the mines. The slave work was hard enough, and adding to this misery, served no earthly purpose. Don Rimado knew this Adolfo would have to be controlled.

FATHER DOMINIC

I N ONE OF the outer buildings behind the church, Sal and
Marianna shared a large room. Each had a cot to sleep on.
This was far better than the mats at the mine. The Father did not
seem to care that they shared the same meager quarters. He was not
concerned with their sexuality. He did not give this any thought. He
saw them as children. He was concerned for their safety. He was only
concerned that they bar the door at night to protect them from further
recruitment by more unscrupulous men.

Salvatore and Marianna did not think about their own sexuality
as they bathed in the fountain in the courtyard in the middle of the night.
They dropped their scant robe and loin cloth with no embarrassment. It
was a secondary thought that nakedness might be of any importance after
laboring so harshly day after day. This was Salvatore's first experience
with a naked woman since he reached puberty. Marianna had seen
plenty of naked boys. She saw them as brothers toiling in the same sweat
canyons as she did. Watching her rinsing her hair and standing with
an unintended seductive pose, as the water ran over the small curves of
her body, his body reacted naturally. It was then that Salvatore began
to see her beauty. She was petite with the gentle curves of beginning

development. When he touched her gently, she felt his heart through his hands. They were now best friends against all the hatred around them. They saw Father Dominic as their savior and felt a relief from the anger of other men. This cemented their feeling for one another. They stood, and bathed in the moonlight of the courtyard, as two innocent young lovers. Without the sulfur coating their bodies, they embraced, feeling clean skin, a sensation, as foreign to them as a new language. After several days they became lovers for life. Their love for one another was more powerful than that driven exclusively by sexuality. Their bonding was born from survival for each other. It was created from the ability to face the harshness of the world together and create something out of nothing. They were two virgin children that had become adults before their time. Flowers and fancy clothes held no sway in this relationship. It was strictly endearment of the purest kind.

I am you and you are me, and together we are one against all who would seek to harm us.

This was their unspoken creed. It was understood by both of them.

They asked Father Dominic if it was possible for him to marry them. Father thought that it was not possible, especially for those so young, to be married in the eyes of the church. He prayed upon this, and then he told them that the Saints had given their permission. It is suspected that the priest allowed his personal emotions and fondness for these teenagers to overwhelm his decision; however, he was going to do it within the secret confines of the church. It would be the two of them along with a witness. This witness was an elderly man who was a caretaker at the church and the cemetery. Early the next day, all four met at the altar. They were the only ones present at six in the morning. Father took their confessions quickly and gave them communion. Neither Marianna nor Salvatore was very sure of what all of the ceremonies were about, but if it was good enough for Father Dominic, it was good enough for them. After they embraced before the Lord, Father blessed and hugged them both. He wondered what the future would bring for these newlyweds.

THE LETTER

AFTER TWO WEEKS, a note was received from Don Rimado.

Father Dominic read the letter to Salvatore and Maria at the evening meal.

Ciao il mio buon amico Padre Dominic-

It has taken me some time to investigate all sides of this incident.

*Since Adolfo is a nephew of a close associate of mine,
I must not punish him too harshly or reduce his station in the Famiglia.
I am going to reassign him to my father's farm near Mt. Etna,
where he will work as a foreman.*

*I must return to France because my father is gravely ill.
Before I go, I will finish dealing with this touchy situation this
fool Adolfo has created.*

First, I must extend my complete apologies to both Marianna and Salvatore. I know how hard they have worked in the mine to earn their keep and repay the debt their families have incurred. I have complete respect for this effort. The mine owners do not want bad publicity. Because of the above conditions and those that follow, please keep the following instructions between ourselves. Sal and Marianna are to be turned over to a man named Ernesto Terzi and be indentured servants to him. This is a long journey to Southwest Sicily but you will be rewarded handsomely. A man named Vero, a shop owner in the marketplace will help with this transition to the Terzi farm. He will meet you half-way on the road. This will ease your journey somewhat, Father. In return, Vero will receive a break on payments to do business. At the present moment, he owes too much. This will allow us to ease his problem with the Mafioso. As you see, Sicily is shaped like a triangle, and we have a triangle here, the rulers, the owners, and the ordinary peasants. As a French-Sicilian noble man, I have tried to be fair in all matters. It is not always so easy to make amends and friendships, or at least, working relationships, between the money, and all concerned.

Le sardine mangiano sempre le acciughe.*

To make this happen I had to make one important and unfortunate conciliatory consolation to the mine owners. After three years, at Terzi's farm, Salvatore must return to the mine and work off his debt. Most importantly, the debt is now heavy, and it will probably take the rest of his life in the Miniera Di Zolfo. They have a choice of either Marianna or Salvatore. I am sure that Salvatore will volunteer himself, as I know that he is a courageous and strong young man. I will see that he gets a promotion at the mine and is allowed a station in life that commands some respect. I extend my greatest apologies for this, but it is the only way we can make it work fairly for everyone involved.

Sincerely, Don Rimado

In the three years that followed Marianna and Salvatore worked very hard for Terzi and gave him no trouble. In fact, he grew to love the young couple and the boys, Samuel and Benedetto. They were born two years apart. The boys grew young and healthy on the farm. After a few years, Vero was a regular visitor and often had Sam come and help him at his trading depot on the coast.

One year after Ben was born, Salvatore returned with an escort of the *Mafia* to the mines. He did not go quietly, or without resistance. Inwardly, he knew he had to hold up his end of the bargain. He fought hard anyway, severely injuring one of the escorts. They would deal with him when they were away from the family. Salvatore was pleased that Marianna was free forever, and his two sons were safe with her. It was the last the boys or Marianna were ever to see of Salvatore.

(A Sicilian phrase that literally translates to "the sardines eat the anchovies". Which loosely means the big fish eat the little ones and further—that's the way life is so you have to live with situation.)

BENEDETTO 1902

THE SICILIAN SUN filtered through the morning mist. It worked its shadows down the vineyard rows that paralleled each other, like an undulating carpet over the rolling hills. Workers would soon be filling baskets full of clusters of the sweet, luscious purple grapes. Harvest time was near. On one side of the vineyard, in an open field, sat a small servant's cottage, a small tool shed, and further on, a horse barn. These were the only buildings except for Terzi, the overlord's casa, which stood majestically in white stucco, in a sharp contrast to nearly everything green around it. It was built upon the largest hill, rising from the valley floor. In the distance, the purple and brown hues of the mountains created a soft background as in a painting. Soon, a cascade of white would adorn these peaks as the fall gave way to winter.

Bennedetto was up early and sat on a bench outside his family's cottage. Ben thought to himself as he gazed into the distance.

Chi beddu paisi! (what beautiful country!)

Ben loved *l'odor del mattino, e odor dei campi, la freschezza dell'aria.* (the smell of the morning, the fields, and the coolness of the air). He rose and walked by his mother's window and saw her still and asleep. He did not wish to wake her.

*Ah **momma, si lavora troppo**. Yesterday you worked too hard in the fields. Terzi should pay you more.*

Ben always thought his mother was treated too harshly. He was very defensive toward anyone that would take advantage of her. In a sense all members of his family were indentured servants from as long as he could remember. Most of the pay from taking care of the horses or working the vineyards and fields was used to pay rent and eat. This was all of life that he knew. Ben grew up entirely without a father. ***No padre***. Ben's father went back to work in the sulfur mines to pay off the remainder of the family debt. This left Ben with many uncertainties in his life. But these empty spaces were filled up with the love of his mother, Marianna. She and his older brother, Sam, were the ones to whom he pledged his life's total being. It was more than just loyalty for his mother. She was the one person he would stand up to anyone for. She was the one who drove him and his brother Sam to become the best young men that they could be.

The fact that Terzi was his "boss" did not bother Benedetto. Ben was a team player and enjoyed whatever task it was that needed to be completed. Chores were merely a way of life for Ben. He did not need "things" to make him happy. He was as comfortable as could be in his old working clothes and was not interested in fancy or showy things. His clothing consisted of short wool pants with a pair of red suspenders. His shirt was loose and pure white. His mother made this for him with all of the love she could bestow with her hands. He had high boots. His socks ran half way up his calves. With his flat black woolen hat, (his cappo), he looked like a mountain man. Ben was thin, but strong and fast. He was very good with a rope and loved to tend to the horses. Ben would do whatever work Terzi assigned him.

Terzi genuinely liked this boy, who was barely a teenager. He became like an uncle to the boy. Not every member, or those who worked for the ***Mafia*** were bad people. Many had good intentions, and only served ***la famiglia*** as a way of survival. It allowed one to live comfortably on the backs of others. One had to pay some for the protection or the position. Many Sicilians did not like this arrangement, but others understood, and accepted it as a way of life.

Many Sicilians did not have any work at this time. *Il raccolto*, (the harvest), was poor because of the blight upon the grapes. Mysteriously, something was killing the crops. However, at harvest time all hands were sorely needed, and all hands became sore.

Ben went back into the *cucina* and broke off a small piece of *pane* and wet it with few drops of water from the sink. He sprinkled some sugar on it and stuffed it in his shirt pocket. Taking a small piece of bread for himself, he strode out the door and across the dirt road, to the field. At the horse barn, Elsa was already waiting for him. She stomped the wooden floor of the stall. Her big grey head nuzzled Ben's hand.

Buongiorno Elsa, let's let the boys out first.

He opened the stall doors and the two young *stalloni*, a small burro, and a mule went racing out across the meadow. He led the big mare out and tied her to a post. There, he began to brush her down. Later he would prepare and hitch her to the buckboard. Terzi would bring his wife to town today. It was the big day for the market. The harvest was poor and his produce would bring a high price. Terzi would be happy. His wife would be delighted as well, for then she would have the money to spend in the shops.

Elsa, I think you like to go to town. Even Terzi gives you a treat sometimes. You think I am too hard on Terzi? Si lavora anche per lui. (you work for him also.) He takes care of our family, but we work hard on the fattoria (farm) too—eh?

The horse nudged Ben's shirt pocket and Ben pulled out the bread for her.

You might have thought that I forgot you? Never—no, no, no—Ben always remembers Elsa. You will look good pulling the cart today. Maybe Terzi will let me ride on the back if there is room. I want to see my brother today. Maybe he has a few minuti for lunchtime.

While he was brushing Elsa down, Ben looked longingly at the hills and the mountains beyond. While many of the young men, including his brother Sam, were men of the sea, Ben longed for the hills. He knew many of the trails leading up to the **Sicanian Mountains**. Beyond that sat Mt Etna, that rose from the landscape with smaller hills all around her. There were places there, even caves, where he could disappear for days at a time. Soon Etna would have a snowy peak. Lately, he had been busy with the farm, but perhaps he could persuade Terzi to let him go tramping for a day. It was then that he noticed a figure in the shadow of the dirt road, that led to the hills.

As he turned towards the cottage, he saw the man sitting on his horse, some distance away. The man looked as though he were out for a ride, but there was a sinister look to him that bothered young Benedetto. Why was he wearing clothing that looked more like a fine suit that one would only wear to weddings, funerals, or church? Ben pretended not to stare back at the man who must have been twice his age. He noticed his mustache and beard, as well as his brown, derby hat. He would ask his mother, or perhaps Terzi, about the man.

After Ben finished brushing Elsa down, he gently slapped the mare on the rump, and she bounded across the field.

His mother was up and making some fried dough. It was a treat breakfast for Ben. He gave her a hug and she summoned him to the table. She noticed a troubled look on his face. When a Sicilian does not speak, his face can read as a mirror into his soul. Ben was not his usual, jubilant self.

Ah, what is on your mind? You seem upset.

Mamma, look out the side window, but do not show your face. Do you see a man watching us from the road? Chi vidi?

His mother, wiped her hands on her apron and looked for a few seconds without care. Then she froze momentarily as if some visage of the past jogged her demeanor. She walked back and sat at the table and stared down at her apron, and then up at her son.

That is a bad, bad man, Benedetto.

She called him by his full name, when she really wanted to gain his attention.

You must be careful of this man.

When Ben started to question, she quickly stopped him.

Listen to me. He works for some other people that you do not need to know.

Marianna had tears of fear in her eyes. Ben was concerned and went to her.

Momma, what is the matter? Who is this man? Why is he watching us? Mi talia. (He looks at me.)

Marianna shrugged her shoulders.

Ti canusci. (He knows you.) Please stay inside the cottage with me Ben. Do not go outside—Stay here with me.

Mamma, why are you so afraid? And—How does he know me?

Ben did not wait for an answer.

I am going to talk to him. I have no fear of this man.

Before his mother could stop him, Ben was out the door and walked directly towards the stranger.

Is there something you need here? Why have you stopped next to our home?

The man did not seem fazed by Ben's direct attitude.

The man responded with an air of indifference and cockiness.

This is a free road for everyone, no? My name is Adolfo. Et tu?

Ben was still perturbed and perplexed.

Si, this is a free road, and I am asking you nicely, to use it and move on.

Adolfo laughed.

Is that how you speak to your elders?

Ben responded sternly. He was showing his anger and his youth.

Only those I distrust.

Ah, like all Sicilians, you don't trust anyone, eh?

No, I don't trust you! Why are you spying on us? What reason is it that you have to watch us? This is mi famiglia.

Adolfo pulled back his riding coat with hands on his hips. There, Ben could clearly see a *pistola* in a shoulder harness. Beyond, Ben saw a long coach whip, black, coiled upon the saddle of his horse. On the man's face, he saw a crooked nose, and dark set eyes, that spoke to him in an unfamiliar silent language of hatred. The stranger spoke.

All of this country—we would be better off if we were one big famiglia—don't you agree paisano?

Look, this is Terzi's land, and I am hired by him to watch over it. So be gone with you and your horse. And, by the way, I am not your paisano.

Adolfo turned and started walking his horse. He began muttering under his breath.

Such big words from such a little man—Tali patri, tali figghiu, (like father, like son)

Ben whirled around.

What did you say?

Adolfo cast a sinister grin over his shoulder and mounted the horse.

I said that it is a beautiful day for a ride. Arrivedercci Ben. Andiamo.

As he rode off in to the distance, Ben stared after him a long time.

For the next few weeks, there was no sign of him, which set Ben's mind at ease. Marianna was still worried because she knew of the past. She knew things that young Ben did not know. The loss of her husband, Ben's father, was still haunting. The darkest days of the past came forward again, into full memory. Someday she would tell Ben everything. He was still much too young.

SAM

IT WAS 1902, and the shipping docks in southwest Sicily were active with traders. However, the economy was poor and agrarian. Profits were limited to few. The peasants struggled to survive. Many Sicilians were leaving for America. It was the highest emigration of people from a small area of land at the time. For example, the number of immigrants to America was twice that of Ireland. The best mode of transportation was by ship. Some were ships with huge sails, but the largest exportation came with steamships. Both frequented the harbors. The world was changing quickly, and often the docks were dangerous places. Men and women from every race, and religious persuasion, populated Sicily. Sicily was a crossroad for Christians, Jews, and Muslims alike. The history of the island includes most every nation that surrounds it. Throughout the centuries, it was home to famous scientists and mathematicians. Since North Africa was geographically close by water across the Mediterranean, it was not unusual to see a Tunisian fisherman trading for olives or lemons with a native Sicilian. They would frequent the many seaports. They dealt with underworld characters, and Sicily was full of the *mafia*. Like every organization, they had their good and bad actors. The mafia was part of Sicilian life, but many of the local people, especially small business owners, hated them. The shop owners had to pay a price to do business. If they refused they were not part of the family. If you were not a part of the family, often you mysteriously disappeared.

The ships stopped for produce. Lemons, oranges, grapes, olives and olive oil, almonds, figs, and many other items were all over the docks to be loaded. Since the palazzo was only a street away, the sailors rejoiced in the opportunity to get their legs on dry land. They often traded with goods from Greece or Africa. Sometimes these goods were human. The language barriers were often crossed with hand signals. Often, the men on the docks were polyglots. Through many languages they understood enough of each tongue to manage the trades.

On one of the loading platforms, a young man, in his late teens, was off loading crates of lemons. He was less than six feet tall but he had a chunky and muscular body. He had a belly like a *barrique* (barrel). As he lifted the last crate from *il carro*, (the cart), he noticed a familiar buckboard. It was Terzi. Then he saw his younger brother Ben, running towards him.

Sam! Sam! I haven't seen you for days. Momma wants to see you.

I know. We have been busy and Vero has been letting me sleep in the wine cellar. That way, he can work me more hours, and I get more pay too. Come e` mamma?

She is tired but she is in good spirits. When I left today, she asked me to see how you were doing.

Terzi took the buckboard and moved on to the market and told Ben that he would catch up with him later in the afternoon. He gave Ben a small amount of money and told him to enjoy himself.

Sam smiled at Ben. See, Terzi does not treat us so bad. We have a place to stay, I have a good job, and now you have some extra money.

At that moment, across the way, some men were grunting at one another, and a crowd had gathered. Sam and Ben walked over to see what the commotion was about. Two men were playing a game called the "stick". It was a contest, in which men sat on the ground, placed their feet together and grabbed a stick between them. When the match started, each man would try to throw the other man over his head. Often, the men would grunt and pull the stick for a long time before one got the advantage over the other. A rather large, burly man with a beard, who looked like one of the sailors from the middle east, gave a huge heave ho and threw his opponent over his head. The smaller man splayed out on the dock and blood gushed from his nose where his face hit first.

The people that gathered cheered and the winner's backer grabbed several coins from the onlookers who bet against his man. A man bumped up against Sam and excused himself.

How would you like to try lad? You look quite stout.

What the man did not know, was that Sam was really good at this game. He had played it before. Ben knew his brother was good as well, because they often talked about these contests. Young Ben tried to encourage his brother to try.

No Ben, I am exhausted. I have been working since sun up and I am hungry and tired.

Ben would not take Sam's answer. He turned to the man with the money.

How much do you want to bet?
How much do you have young man?
I have two hundred. Ben was lying.
Two hundred it is. Let's get the contest moving on here.

Before anyone knew what was happening, Sam was lined up with his opposition. This was a large man with big rippling muscles under all the fat that he carried. Sam braced himself.

One of the men of the dock started the contest fairly and then whistled. You could see the beginning effort was tremendous. It showed on both of the contestants' faces. Sam turned and gave Ben a look of disdain for getting him into this. The people on the docks had often seen Sam stick wrestle before and they knew he was good at it. He became affectionately known as "The Bull". Someone in the crowd saw that the stalemate needed some encouragement, so he started a chant.

The Bull! Il Toro! The Bull! The chanting continued and slowly the tide began to turn against Sam. The big man was gaining on him! Ben started yelling.

You can't lose Sam. Pull him over. Come on Sam.

Deep in his heart Sam knew his brother did not have the money to bet and if he should lose this contest, they were both in big trouble. He began to increase his effort. He saw the older fat man begin to tire. He could feel it. The man began to call Sam filthy names. The man began to sweat and furl his brow. Somehow, Sam kept the pressure enough to let the man know that he was losing the psychological battle. Sam quietly whispered to the man whose face was less than a foot from his.

Did your mother teach you those dirty words?

The man did not have a chance to respond. In that instant, he flew over Sam's head onto the dock. He came up swinging and Sam scrambled to his feet and ducked. At that moment he grabbed the money out of the betting man's hand and he yelled to Ben to run. The crowd held the beaten man back and the boys were gone.

Sam—you did it!

Sam grabbed his brother and threw him into the dirt.

If you ever do that again, I will let those men have their way with you. I will throw you off the pier.

Ben rolled over in the dirt and laughed. He knew his brother would get over it. Sam was the "Bull" but Ben thought he was the gambler, and the brains of the family. In reality, Ben was the mischievous little brother that you either hated or loved. Sam loved his younger brother even if he thought Ben was smarter. However, Ben was a gambler, and that would stay with him the rest of his life.

Sam was two years older, but Ben had a great mind for numbers. He could compute large numbers in his head although he did not yet know how to write them. He had great facility for learning new languages and sounds, but he could not read nor write. This was a boy that learned about people's personalities and was able to win over hearts easily. He was what one would call a people person. He was not educated as a book learner, but learned in the ways of people actions and emotions. He had a crafty intelligence and was wise to a person's intentions. What he did not know on paper, he knew in reality. The experience would soon come naturally.

VERO

YEARS OF HARD labor on the docks and running three businesses did not show on Vero's body. He still looked a younger-aged man although he was approaching fifty. He was a cooper, a produce trader, and a vintner. His close proximity to the docks in the harbor town of Trapani, made his building a valuable piece of real estate. Handed down in his family for four decades, it was natural that the only son carried forward with the trade. The mafia left him alone as he paid his share of ransom. He did not like it, but accepted it due to the fact that he hid much of his profit from them. What they didn't know, they didn't know. Many of his deals with shippers and farmers were off the books. This was a way of life in Sicily.

As the years progressed, he became a central figure in the town because he could fix any wagon that was broken down. He could recommend an injured mariner to the nearest doctor for an illness. He was able to broker deals between different shippers and often, the goods never hit shore. They just passed from ship to ship and he collected a fee for the transaction. Often, these goods were traded this way to avoid a fee to the government, or to an inspector. The officers in charge of the pier were also friends with Vero. Many of them were in that position because of his recommendation or "suggestion". This is the way business was transacted, fast and easy, with money exchanged quickly, with little conversation. Sometimes, it was just a slip of paper, like a numbers game. None of this diminished the likeability of Vero, but rather enhanced it. The men of the dock had a certain respect for each other and the merchants. This was the way they had made their living for centuries. The Arabs, Greeks, Spaniards, French, and Northern Europeans, all spoke some of each other's languages. This is why Sicily was the crossroads of languages and the root of the romance languages. It was also home to the famous poets, scientists, and mathematicians. All of Sicily was filled with philosophers. It seems that every Sicilian was a philosopher unto his own.

Vero, a burly man, with a powerful build, and long, curly, salt and pepper hair, usually had a broad smile and affable way about him. His wire rimmed spectacles, would make you think he was a professor, or a Galileo type, in another setting. Certainly, his facility with numbers, and calculations that he could do in his head, would tell you that he was a brilliant man. So this man was a central figure for the mini-universe of Western Sicily. There was much that he knew about everyone and everything.

Vero loved the family of Ben and Sam, and especially Marianna. He knew Marianna's husband, Salvatore, the father of Ben and Sam, many years before. They were best friends. It was he, Vero, who helped broker the deal to save Marianna and Salvatore from the mines. He dealt with a Don Rimado and a priest named Father Dominic. Together, they had saved a family. It was then that he looked for Salvatore's parents and sister, but finally, was convinced that they had emigrated to the Americas. His unique position at the port, allowed him to find answers, when silence was a motto among the population.

When Salvatore, disappeared, he went looking for him. It did not take him long to find out that he was disposed of by the Mafia. Vero was too late to help him. Sal was a guy that took no guff from anyone, lest somebody trying to rob him of his hard earned crops and money he was saving for his sons. Sal was a rough character, but no man is a match for a well-aimed piece of lead. Sal did not have a pistol, and fought bravely with his bare hands. This is the way it was for many Sicilian farmers. They showed incredible bravery against men with guns. Many times their weapons were pitchforks or clubs. The absentee landholders, *(the latifondisti)*, from Rome, Turin, Paris, or Barcelona, carried power with their money and soldiers for hire.

After Salvatore was captured and eventually killed, Vero became much more guarded and was careful not to convey too much information about anything to do with his business or the people he dealt with. In this situation, he knew Marianna would have a difficult time raising the boys by herself and asked a favor of Terzi and his wife Anna, to take the family in and let them work on the farm. When the boys were young, they certainly could not do too much, but again Vero covered the cost under the table. He fell in love with Marianna years before but would never have approached her when Salvatore was alive. Now, it was different. From time to time they enjoyed each others' company. The boys were always included and he helped to ease them into life. When Sam was old enough, around eight years of age, he began to train him in the businesses of the Vero family. Sam became like family. Indeed, he could pass for being Vero's son. The younger Ben, stayed on the farm, helped his mother, Marianna, and took care of Terzi's horses and animals. He and his mother also learned much about how to tend to a vineyard and the fruit trees.

Sometimes, Vero would take the boys fishing on his boat that he kept moored for personal use only. These were rare occasions as there was so much work to do. Often, they would catch so many fish that they earned a handsome price from the docks. Vero would let the boys keep all of the money, and sometimes he added some to the coffer without them knowing. It was better to let them think they earned it all. The boys hid this money in a secret place. Under the corner of the cottage, which was made of stone, the boys unearthed one of the stones very carefully. Beneath this stone, there was a small space for a wooden box. In this box, they kept their money. They never went to the money during the day hours when they might be seen, nor did they even tell

Marianna where it was. They did not want her tortured for their money. Most people thought them poor anyway. In this way, they accumulated a good amount of cash. Every other part of their life was consumed with bartering for food or clothing. Sam would always remember the day when his mother cried because he had brought her material from the docks for a new dress. Vero had helped again. Marianna was the matron of the family and Vero became the rock. Terzi helped somewhat, but was handcuffed by the absentee landlords to hand over a high percentage of everything the farm produced.

MARIANNA

As the mother of two boys, Marianna was cautionary. She knew of the man that was watching them. Firsthand experience had taught her well. She did not trust the same men she knew had taken her husband. All of these years, she kept the truth from the boys, because at first, they were too young to know of these things. Now, she wanted to tell them everything, but did not know exactly how. She would confide in Vero and ask him to break the truth to the boys. Vero wanted to help her and was asked many times in the last year, but he had always refused, not knowing how it would affect his relationship with them. He was also, genuinely concerned about their welfare if they should try to do something about it. This was a tricky situation for everyone, not only because of the emotions of the truth, but also the possible consequences of the boys' actions afterwards. She sent a message to Vero via Terzi. It is strange that Marianna felt that she was at fault for all that happened.

Her Salvatore was no longer with her. Vero said, he thought that they had killed him. He was never positive. Salvatore was the first and only true love of her life. She could remember every moment her man stood up to the thug, Adolfo. Brave Salvatore was a huge emotional and real loss for Marianna. If Adolfo had not hit her, maybe her husband would still be alive.

Vero attempted to console her.

The victim often feels this way. You can't blame yourself Marianna!
It was small consolation for her loss.

When she did not have to work the farm, to keep busy, she sewed shirts, and pants, for the boys. When she opened the package Ben and Sam brought home from Vero, she held the fabric in her hands and wept. The brilliant red fabric was laced with white designs. The bolt of cloth had been traded at the docks with a merchant from the north of Europe. He was especially interested in Vero's wines. He made a very good deal and capped it off with the fabric, bartered for some extra barrels that Vero had made. Vero knew she would love the gift. Ben and Sam were proud when they gave her the package.

She was in her late twenties now, and perhaps this new cloth would make her look young again. The mines could make anyone old before their time. Marianna took the cloth and cut it so the white markings bordered the hem. She thought it looked like a Gypsies dress when she finished. With her white blouse and laced black boots, she wondered what the local priest would say when she went to church. Sicilians generally wore black, black dresses, black veils, and black kerchiefs. An extra black scarf around the neck was not unusual. The church felt that everyone should show suffering for Christ. One should always outwardly demonstrate this sorrow. Her demeanor was different than the other women. Marianna had already suffered this sorrow in the mine, many times over. When she became free, her spirit soared. She would wear what she wanted, when, and wherever she wished. That Sunday morning, she proudly walked into the cathedral with her two young men in tow. Marianna, in her new dress, took communion with both boys, one on each side, they knelt at the altar.

She remembered Father Dominic whenever she took the host. She always recalled fondly, the way the old priest would raise the host towards the ceiling of the church. He would be proud of Marianna now, twelve years later, regularly attending mass. She had hardened to life as it was. Life for most Sicilians was extremely difficult, not on the edge of poverty, but living in it.

Seeing her at the altar with her young men, Vero stood well in the back. He looked at the three of them in contrast to all the black dresses and dark clothing around them. He could not help but smile with pride.

What a beautiful woman! Che bella donna!

TUTU

Tutu was picking through his nets and fishing gear in the small harbor. He was on the island of Favignana. This was his new home for the last five years. He moved there with his wife and children from Tunisia. His real name was Abdus Salam, which meant, servant of peace. Tutu became his nickname from a Sicilian fisherman who pulled next to him during a *Mattanza*. This was known as a slaughter of blue fin tuna, which were huge fish. It took strong men to pull the nets over the side of the boat. It may have been in the fervor of the moment when men were yelling out commands, but somehow, *Tutu* was uttered and it stuck. Tutu never minded because it was close to a famous Egyptian King's name.

Favignana is an interesting small island because of its unique topography. It is shaped like a moth or a butterfly. In the middle of where the wings meet is a busy harbor. There were many vessels at anchor and these were mostly fishing boats. They were equipped to handle heavy nets for the most part. This was because of the Tuna runs which were so popular off of this part of Sicily. Also, there were many family farms.

Because of the winds and poor fishing for that day, Tutu anchored overnight in the most protective harbor. Tutu would often make trips as long as a week if he was making good deals between fishing and trading. In short, he would ride with the wind and the tides. He was running along the southern coast of Sicily and the ports of Trapani and Marsala. Sometimes he sailed as far as the Gulf of Castellamare and then back to some fishing grounds off of Mozia.

Looking up at the sky, he wondered if he should set sail this morning. The wind seemed right, but the sky looked as if it might change to a darker more sinister hue by the afternoon. If it did blow and get nasty, he could turn **The Desert Wind** back towards Sicily and Trapani.

Tutu's boat was a nine-meter sailing and rowing craft made out of wood. He had made numerous trips towards Sicily and the coastal towns. When sailing a craft of this size, alone, safety always becomes an issue. He felt at home with the sea. He had spent his entire life crossing the Mediterranean to other ports. Tutu was a good sailor, trader and fisherman. He used all of these skills to make a fine income for himself and this allowed him to provide for his family.

He pushed his craft off the shore and hoisted the mainsail. The sail billowed quickly and **The Desert Wind**, heeled to starboard. He set sail toward Tripani. The waves were off reasonable size, but the sea currents off of Southwest Sicily can be tricky. Close to these islands, many sailors have misjudged the wind, waves, and rocks.

Negotiating around these small islands near the towns of Trapani and Marsala was something Tutu was used to doing. As long as the weather was fair, he was safe. But Tutu was not just a fair weather sailor. He had a strong faith in God. He was a devout Muslim. He believed that Allah had total control of his boat and the seas. His faith was stronger than danger would allow. His own physical and mental strength pushed him to do more than a normal man would consider possible.

He set to dreaming of home, his wife Mira, and his two girls, Amira, and Palika. He thought of his family while he sailed. His wife and two children handled the chores of the small plot of land that he owned. They would be out tending to the garden now. He could see them milking the goats, and gathering the eggs from the chickens. Tutu had few supplies to bring home that were really necessary. The main food supplies he traded for were flour, and the beloved sugar for his daughters. Sometimes he was able to find rare spices. Mira would mix this sugar with a goat cheese called ricotta. This was filling for canola, a type of pastry that Mira learned how to make from the Sicilians on the island. Tutu liked to mix the ricotta in with some home-made pasta and then topped with some sardines or anchovies. Peppers from the garden were added for taste, if available. Some trips he traded for delicious artichokes.

Tutu had made many friends among the islanders. He would not sell all of his fish, but rather bring some to his neighbors. This bonding between fellow islanders, allowed him to take these trips. These bonds that islanders have for one another, have existed since the dawn of civilization. Maybe it is the isolation and limited supply of resources that creates this kind of kinship. He knew his family was well guarded and cared for. Had they lived on mainland Sicily, he was not as sure that this would be the case. When Tutu was in all of these ports he was very wary of strangers, and stayed within the town port. He had seen plenty of unsavory characters in these towns.

He sailed by sight, and when Mount Cofano could be seen in the distance, it was his landmark to turn half-circle down the coast. The tiller was deep and helped because the keel was not the full length of the boat. Tutu found the craft years before, abandoned on the coast of Tunisia. He and a friend resurrected the craft, and modified it to the needs of a fisherman and trader. They increased the sail area which made the boat fast, but also vulnerable to a knock down. Whenever Tutu felt threatened by the extreme heel of the boat, he would simply let out the mainsail and spill wind. The sail had no boom at its foot. Using his right arm and a sheet running through a chock, to control the sail, he steered with his left hand on the tiller. He developed a way to sail this way with a feel of the wind and water through his body. No sailor is better than a sailor who can do this by feel. Tutu was as close to nature and the weather as one could become.

Tutu had a tendency to daydream, as solo sailors often do. This momentary lack of concentration in rough water can spell disaster.

He was racing downwind with his sail as a wing when he heard the bang and scrape that any seaman does not want to hear. The underwater rock ripped through the hull so quickly it left a long gash clear through the decking. Tutu could see the seawater through the opening. Because the craft was now pinned on the rock, the next wave lifted the bow high and then smashed it downward. At the same time, the wind filled the sail, whose sheet became pinned in the chock. The mast became totally submerged and the boat upturned. On the way into the sea, Tutu smashed his head on the gunwale. The boat slid off the rock shelf as a bleary-eyed sailor watched his boat descend to the depths. He then realized that the safety line that he tied around his waist was still fastened. He frantically tried to untie the line but then felt the heavy craft yank him towards the bottom. Tutu finally untied himself and shot towards the surface. As he struggled to stay afloat, he saw his own blood clouding the water all around him. He began to fade.

A BIG FISH

To answer Marianna's wishes, Vero decided that he would take the boys fishing. Even though it was late fall and close to the winter season, they would go for grouper, or other good eating fish. Tuna season was long over. The boys would be a captive audience on the boat, only a nine meter craft. If they became upset or showed too much emotion, it would be a small audience of those that really cared. The brothers were excited about the day and there were many arrangements made. Terzi would watch the horses for the day. The boys would borrow the buckboard for a promise to bring extra fish home for Terzi and Anna. There was no large net needed because they would not be going for Tuna. The boys had helped Vero many times before when the large Tuna were running. They pulled the nets and helped haul the huge fish on board. Some of the tuna ran as much as 100 kilos and up. They were huge fish and blood would be everywhere. This adventure promised to be much cleaner and more enjoyable.

Sam pushed off of the dock. Ben tended the lines and Vero steered. Then Sam settled into the oars. After an hour, Sam switched with Ben as they neared the fishing grounds. They were about five kilometers off shore in the Mediterranean Sea. Bobbing in the waves, they baited the hooks and set their lines. The wind was picking up some, but it did not seem to worry them. Vero began changing the subject from the normal jokes that men tell at sea, to the more serious topic he was to cover. He did not do it very well. Sam and Ben were surprised to see some tears rolling down Vero's face. They had never seen him this way before.

Every time he began to talk, he started to choke up. He was trying to find a way to tell the boys about their father, Salvatore. While Vero was starting the conversation, Ben noticed a sailboat coming towards them, well heeled over to starboard. A single figure was standing in the stern trying to manage the waves which began to mount to the East. It was a fantastic sight to see the bow rise up and come crashing down, sending spray high above the rollers. Vero stopped talking and shouted to pull in the lines and man the oars. Sam was quickly in the seat and Ben was busy tending to the fishing lines. In the next instant the sailboat heading toward them was sinking fast. It was a knock down, and the mast was quickly disappearing below the water line. Ben could just make out the man in the water, less than fifty meters from them. Vero was yelling for Sam to pull hard on the oars in the drowning man's direction. As they neared the man, they could see him struggling to stay afloat, and blood was gushing from a gash in his head. There was no sign of his boat. It was completely gone to the bottom of the sea. Before anything else could happen Ben was in the water with a line, swimming directly at the man. Ben never learned to swim very well. This thought was lost to Ben. He did not even think about that fact because everything happened so quickly. He was without fear of his own safety.

By the time Ben reached him, the man was gasping for air and exhausted. The man began to sink and at the last instant Ben reached below the water and grabbed his thick locks. The sailor pulled Ben under for a moment. Tying the line around his own waist first, Ben grabbed him around his chest and under his arms. He yelled at Sam to pull them in. When they were close to the boat, the boys gave a supreme effort to push and pull him over the gunwale. Vero did all he could to steady the boat into the waves trying to keep the bow from crashing down on the swimmers' heads. With the few words the man was muttering, they could tell he was Tunisian. He was an Arab, with an enormous head of hair. Vero was doing all he could do to calm the man and attend to his wound. He took off his shirt and wrapped it around the man's forehead. He kept dousing the wound with salt water to rinse away the blood and keep it clean. Soon they would be inside the bay and calmer waters would prevail.

Sam worked the oars hard and they had the wind at the stern, so they were moving quickly. Instead of beaching the boat, they went straight to the docks which were further on down the bay. Arriving at the docks, a crowd soon gathered wondering what this big "fish" they had in the bottom of the boat was. Their banter turned to serious talk when they realized the man was hurt. Sam and Vero carried the man from the docks to the buckboard and then carted him back to Vero's shop. Ben went to get the doc.

Dr Summarti, affectionately called "Sumo", was there quickly. He told everyone to get out of the room and give him some space to work.

After an hour or so, he came out to see Vero and the boys.

That is a huge man in there. He is breathing fine now. From what little Arabic I know, he thinks you are sent from Allah. You can go in there now, but take it easy on him. He is not ready to walk yet. When you are done let him rest for awhile.

Vero thanked Sumo profusely and gave him a package of goods and a little extra *vino* as payment. He was pleased with that.

NEW FRIENDSHIP

THE THREE FISHERMAN crowded around the bed. The man in the bed slowly opened his eyes until it seemed they were the size of a tuna eyes. They were two huge orbs in the middle of a huge, black face.

The man stared at them and said nothing. He took his index finger and pointed it at his chest and said,

"TUTU". Then louder—*TU—TU.*

The boys began to laugh and pointed to their own chests and called out their names.

Ben! Sam! Ben!

Vero yelled,

Hey—hey—one at a time!!

Tutu spoke in a broken tongue of all sorts, Sicilian, English, French, Spanish, and Arabic. It seemed that every word went from one language to another. The four of them enjoyed the constant banter and finger pointing back and forth. Then Tutu asked about his boat. Vero made a sign like a diving hand—as if to say its long gone to the bottom.

How do you feel about losing your boat, Tutu?

Tutu no sad. Tutu alive! Can get another boat! Can not get another Tutu.

He said this in what seemed every language and dialect possible, and the boys roared with laughter. Then Tutu pointed at Ben.

You save Tutu's life. Tutu forever for you.

As he said this he pounded his chest and poked his finger into Ben's chest. He took Ben's hand and held it in both of his hands. He repeated.

Tutu forever for you.

Vero laughed at Ben.

I think he means that he is indebted to you for helping him.

Ben seemed embarrassed.

Anyone would have done that. You all helped too.

Yeah, but you went in the water. That's a big difference.

What's going to happen to him now?

Vero thought for a moment.

Well, we will have to look after him for a few days. Then we will need to get him back home.

Where is his home?

I think he said Favignana Island. You should bring him out to your mother's place.

Ben responded.

Domani, domaini.

They let Tutu rest for the night.

As Ben dozed off to sleep that night, he tried to put the events of the day together. What was it that Vero wanted to tell him? Why was he so emotional? Ben looked over at Sam. They were sleeping among the wine barrels in Vero's shop. **Hey Sam.**

What?

What do you think Vero was trying to tell us?

Probably how much he loves mom.

Oh yeah! You are probably right! But why is he crying about Momma?

Shut up Ben. Go to sleep.

HOME

T HE NEXT MORNING, Tutu, with both of his arms draped over the shoulders of Ben and Sam, hobbled out to the buckboard. Ben decided to bring Tutu home to rest for at least three or four days, or until he felt well enough to function on his own.

Look, Tutu, when you have rested for a couple of days, I will get you back home on your island.

Tutu had told him where he lived, on the island of Favignana. He could not wait until he was able to go home. He knew that his wife and children would be worried about him. Wives of sailors know that the worst can happen at any time. Vero knew this and sent word by currier that he was all right and resting in Sicily. The captains often did these favors for Vero for they stopped in these ports along the way. The message was that her husband would be home soon, and he was well although the boat was lost.

It took more than two hours to arrive at the cottage and Ben noticed something strange. The door was wide open. Ben called to his mother but there was no answer and when he went inside he saw that there were some cooking utensils on the floor and the kitchen chair was turned over. Ben felt a chill.

Mama-mama!

He looked outside in the pasture and she was not there. He ran to Terzi's house and Anna answered the door.

Have you seen my mother?

Ann shouted to the back of the house, *Emilio!*

Terzi came to the door quickly.

What is the matter?

My mother is gone!

Ben was nearly shaking.

When all had settled down, Terzi, Tutu, and Ben sat in the cottage and decided what to do. Ben's plan was to ride back to Vero's and have his brother join him to go looking for his mother. Terzi thought too much time would be wasted. Ben thought about Tutu as well. Tutu said that he would help and that he felt well enough. This was not what Ben had planned for the big fisherman, but Tutu would not take no for an answer. So finally it was decided that Terzi would ride and tell Sam. Sam would bring a buckboard and some camping supplies and meet Ben at a cave they both knew how to find. This plan was made so he and Tutu could gain some ground. There was no doubt which direction they took his mother in. Ben had a good idea that it was Adolfo. Ben could see the wagon tracks in the soft dirt. It looked like they took a mountain road and it was headed straight East. Ben knew these roads well. He knew them better than his brother. Ben would ride a small stallion, and Tutu, Elsa. Tutu said he knew horses well and had no problems riding. They did not have a pistol, but they had knives and clubs.

Tutu looked at Ben. Tutu asked if he could look around in the shed and Ben waved him to go ahead. As he walked away, Ben could not help but marvel at the size of the man. He also was taken by his confidence. Tutu acted as if he were a warrior returned from many successful battles. Maybe he was.

Ben's thoughts returned to his mother. He knew she was a tough woman, but these men could be mean. He did not want to lose her as he had no father. That would leave him without any parents. His connection to the world was through Vero, Sam, and his mother. That was it. Sam was the older brother, but his mother always spent more time with Ben. That's because he lived with her every moment of every day. Sam was busy working on the docks with Vero, and might come home every few days. This left a strong bond between Ben and his mother. He would find her. He had to find her.

Tutu returned from the back yard shed.

Do not worry little brother, Tutu know how to fight. Tutu kill many men in the desert of Africa, many years ago. I am feeling better now.

Ben showed concern and wondered if Tutu should go at all.

I am worried about that gash in your head and whether you are well enough to ride.

Do not worry Bennie Boy—This Tutu like stone. I find this in your shed and I make it sharp!

Tutu held up a curved machete that was like a razor and a meter long.

Ben looked at Tutu. This massive African man looked as if he could break a man's bones with his bare hands. Since Ben was so young, he did not mind having a man like this with him at all. His brother Sam would be worried, but when all three met up at the cave, they would have a small army among them.

Along the road towards the cave, Ben and Tutu found some red cloth on the roadway. When they saw a second piece, they knew it was Marianna, showing them they way. Ben was heartened by this. It meant that they were not wasting time, traveling in the wrong direction. It was no doubt that it was the same material they had given her, because it had some white markings on it, and the pattern was unmistakable. She was not leaving large pieces, just enough to find the way.

ADOLFO

MARIANNA WAS GAGGED and her wrists and ankles were tied tightly with rope. It was hours before they stopped and her face and neck were badly bruised from the heaving buckboard.

Her dress was torn and she was sore and weary from her battle with Adolfo. The twenty-eight year old woman had fought valiantly. Marianna was hardened from her work in the vineyards and she hatred the intruder. These things made the capture difficult. She might have bested the beast but the *pistola* would have ended it anyway. The cowardly animal would have had to save face and he would have killed her. If she had not hit her head on the table when pushed violently to the floor, she would have at least extended the fight. She wanted Ben to know that she did not go willingly. She hoped someone would rescue her, as she rolled around on the back of the cart. She was able to tear small pieces of her dress from the hem, even though her hands were tied. She would push them off the back of the wagon with her feet. Adolfo had taken her boots off as well. It seemed that Adolfo hit all the stones and holes in the road on purpose. She knew she would be forced to work as a slave in the fields and probably worse. She did not want to go back to the sulfur mines. That memory was etched in her psyche forever. The fact that she was alive gave her hope.

He stopped the horse and came back to look at Marianna. Adolfo could not help himself. He had to make a wise remark.

Hello Marianna.

The ride is comfortable, no?

He laughed sarcastically. He tilted his head to look directly into her face. If not gagged, she would have spit into his face.

We will stop here for the night. Do not give me any trouble or you will pay dearly.

He grabbed her by the ankles and yanked her out of the wagon. As her head hit the ground first, she heard the ringing of bells behind her eyes. He dragged her feet first behind some trees, just off the road. Her skirt was around her face and Adolfo enjoyed the full view of her nakedness.

Maiale! Maiale! (pig-pig)

Adolfo could only hear muffled cries through the gagged mouth.

I do not care about your pain woman, but I do not want to kill you. You treat Adolfo nice, and he treat you nice too eh?

If she were too beat up or wounded, she would be of no use. If he wanted to be paid for bringing her in, he needed to ease up on the punishment.

Marianna was tough and rugged for her thin, small frame. She was struggling to survive against this brute. In a small grove of trees, Adolfo leaned her up against a boulder. He untied her gag rag. She was quick to speak.

You animal! You will die for this! Morte per voi! You know I have children to take care of. We have a deal with Don Rimado. We have paid our debt. Why are you still involved with us? You should leave us alone. Let me go and I promise I will never bother you again.

Adolfo thought for a moment.

You caused me great pain woman. When Father Dominic reported that I beat you and Salvatore, I was demoted. I was sent to watch over Don Rimado's father's farm. So my life is no better than the peasants I command. I deserve better. You are no better than a common peasant Marianna. So I will treat you like one. I can beat you again and again and bend you to my will. Even if your boys come after you, I will be waiting for them, eh? The pistol is master of all. You can beg and plead all you want. I have no sympathy for you or your dead husband. Maybe it was me that killed your beloved Salvatore eh? You will never know.

Marianna looked at him with fire in her eyes.

Was it my husband that gave you that crooked nose or that dent in your head? No wonder you are so stupid. You are just a dumb man with no love in your heart for anyone. I bet you don't even have a dog that likes you.

This did not bother Adolfo. He had heard plenty of threats before, from the other women he had captured, and plenty of men too. He felt that this little woman could do him no harm. He went about his business, hiding the horse and wagon away from the road. Then he built a small fire and made some coffee. He offered some to Marianna and she spat it into his face. She caught a wicked backhand for this.

The temperature was dropping because of the altitude. Adolfo wrapped himself in his bed roll. Marianna was not so fortunate. As the fire died down to embers, her body began to shake. As her captor fell off to sleep, she tried to loosen the rope around her wrists. If her hands were tied in front of her body, she could have used her teeth. She had an idea. By crouching into a fetal position, she was able to pull her hands under her butt and slide her legs through the loop made by her arms. She put her back to the fire and chewed on the rope. After a long time, she finally loosened her wrists. They were raw and bleeding but they were free! In little time she untied her ankles. Marianna moved ever so slowly away from the embers of the dying fire and into the night.

She stood there for several minutes, looking at Adolfo. She was thinking that she might kill him. How would she do that? She would be rid of this man forever. She could not understand why he was so mean—even to children. If she thought she could have succeeded in killing him this night by any means possible, she would have done it. Instead, she began inching her way away from the camp.

THE CHASE

B EN AND TUTU did not know how far ahead the wagon was but they could close ground quickly by horseback. Tutu was on big Elsa and Ben rode the young stallion. Elsa being more calm, would help to keep the stallion in a better riding mood. Tutu looked like a giant upon Elsa. He was the African warrior and gave an air of no fear. Not knowing how much trouble they would run into, Ben was happy to be with Tutu at his side. At first, they covered ground quickly, but as the roads became steep, they slowed to an even pace.

Soon they came to the place to leave the road and take the trail. It was a short cut and it was steep. When the sun started to fall below the horizon, they stopped and made camp. It still would be a day's ride but it was good that they proceeded slowly. Tutu's head needed to heal. The mare was surprisingly gentle on Tutu's body and the day went without incident. Around the fire, they discussed what they thought might have happened to Marianna. They discussed all of the possibilities and the actions they might take. Tutu sharpened his machete while sitting by the fire. Ben studied his hands and the way they held the big sharp blade. It made a formidable weapon in his hands. Ben did not know what the next days would bring, but he did not care. Ready or not, he would fight for his mother. Anything might happen as these were bad times, and ruthless men who would do anything to gain an advantage.

Ben spoke first.

Tutu, I think we should wait at the cave for Sam. Then the three of us will spy upon the plantation that has taken her. I am pretty sure of where it is. On one of my tramps, I walked for many days and saw these vineyards way on the other side of the Sicandia Mountains. We are in this mountain range. The vineyards and orchards are in the foothills near Etna. Etna already has snow on her peak. I saw it yesterday through one of the ranges. We have a long way to go. Near there, maybe a day's ride, we will find the cave. It is where Sam and I used to go on our overnight adventures in to the wilderness. From the cave, we will ride during the night and spy on this farm. Vero will know where it is. I think he has been there. Maybe it is just one nights ride from the cave. We can find out how many men are there and how many workers.

Tutu listened intently on every word and then replied.

Tutu hear you well little one. But Tutu know how to fight better without horse. Must be quiet. No sound. We surprise men. We take only machete and club. We take water. That is all. We get your mamma.

Ben thought Tutu said it so simply that it sounded easy. He wasn't so sure. The only thing he did know was that he was happy Tutu was on his side. Ben had never done any serious fighting with anyone. It wasn't that he was afraid. Quite the contrary, he was brave, but bravery does not cancel out uncertainty. Ben stared at the machete gleaming in the firelight and wondered, and wondered. An anxious young man prayed for his mother. A man, nearly twice his size was already sleeping in his bedroll.

FLIGHT

MARIANNA WAS BAREFOOT which made walking on the rocky ground difficult. The many scrapes, cuts, and bruises were one thing, but the pain of walking in these hills was a problem. She would have to hike on the road to gain some distance between Adolfo and her. She thought the road would take her back down if she followed it. It was also the easiest way for her to be caught. She had to think but her brain was bashed as much as her body. It would be great if someone would find her on this road, a lonely traveler perhaps. On this road, at night, in the mountains, there was little hope. Ben and Sam will be looking for me. Perhaps I should leave them some signs. She decided to rip a piece of her red dress off. Tearing it into strips, she tied these to trees along the roadway. She also knew she was giving away her position to Adolfo. She was taking that chance. She must continue to give signs to her sons to follow.

She found a small clearing and another road that descended. She ripped more of her dress away and wrapped the fabric around her feet. This was a great comfort to the toes and soles of her feet. Now she could move more quickly with less pain. She thought back to the sulfur mines and how much her feet hurt when she carried the ore.

She remembered how the pain began to dull, when day after day, the monotonous, tortuous cave floor tore at her feet. She thought about her beloved Salvatore and what Adolfo had just revealed to her. She felt certain that it was this Adolfo who was responsible for her husband's death, if he was indeed dead. She had no reason to doubt this. She had not seen her husband from the time of Ben's birth. That was twelve years ago. In her heart, Salvatore had passed on. Maybe it was better that way. He did not have to endure the mines, nor the torture any more. He had served his lot in life. She knew that he loved his two beautiful sons. She snapped back to the moment, angry with herself for daydreaming. She must concentrate.

She heard something in the distance at the bottom of a meadow. It was a small stream dropping and gurgling through the gorge. Here the field of grass ran straight up to the stream and then a towering rock wall bordered the water from the opposite side. There was a path that she could see more clearly when l'alba della loce, (the early dawn light) came. She could not scale the sides of the canyon which grew even more steeply as she progressed down the path. In this part of Sicily, there were many canyons and stream beds. Some had water in them and at this time of year, there were many dry gullies as well. As she shuffled and stumbled forward, she was shocked as the path abruptly ended. A huge stone wall stood before her with no way up or around. This is where the stream fell into a large pool and then rocketed over a precipice to boulders far below. On her right side was an opening through the rock, which she squeezed into and then through. The narrow way opened into a vineyard. A vineyard! The grapes in these mountains were the last to be harvested. Marianna's luck was turning. She snatched a clump from the nearest vine and shoved them into her mouth. She ate as fast as she could for a few minutes, until the juice ran down her face and hands. The sweet fruit gave her strength and resolve, but she was tired. She walked back to the opening in the rock, and stripped off all of her clothes. She studied the pond for a moment. There seemed to be no danger. Goosebumps erupted over her naked skin as she slid into the pond. *Freddo-freddo!* Once she was used to the cold, she rubbed herself to wash the caked and dried blood from every part of her body. It was then that she discovered the cross of Jesus was still around her neck. She kissed it and thanked the Lord for being alive. Father Dominic had given this to her after mass one morning. She wished the good father was with her at this moment. Then she remembered what the priest had told her. Jesus is with you in your hours of greatest need. She always doubted but then reaffirmed her faith. It was always a give and take with the Lord. She remembered how Salvatore would joke with her during the evening meals.

How could he have found humor in such a painful time?

Maybe that was the Lord working through Salvatore. Marianna left it at that. Why worry about things that she had no control over? She rinsed her hair several times over until she was satisfied that she was clean.

The sun dried her quickly as it was now mid-morning. She dressed and rewrapped her feet in the cloth as before. She edged along and hid behind the vineyard rows until she found a small tool shed. She saw no one about. Inside, she found hanging, some old work pants and a hat. In the corner, a pair of work boots were lined up neatly under a shelf. She quickly tried them on. They were a couple of sizes too big. She stuffed some of the cloth pieces into the toes and found that they would do. She thought,

I must look a sight. I will move quickly now and rest later.

She climbed out of the vineyard and found another path. This path was winding and rising into switchbacks. Before she knew it, the air was cooler again, and she was half way up a small mountain. She knew she could not go this way and doubled back down to the vineyard. On the other side of the vineyard was a small hill. She would try that. She was confused and lost.

END OF THE ROAD

S HE KNEW SHE could not travel further by the stream
because of the canyon. She decided to find the road again.
By following the vineyard rows she eventually came to the top of a hill
that gave her a good vantage point. In the distance she could see an
expanse of blue. It was the Mediterranean Sea! Now she realized that
the road must run to the southern side of the mountains. If she followed
it, she would be able to find one of the coastal towns. From there she
could get home. She started down this road, all the while, looking over
her shoulder. There were very few trees now as the way opened on to a
wide expanse of rocky, barren wilderness. She walked for what seemed
hours. The late afternoon sun was baking her and she looked for shade.
Finally, she crossed a small stream, and drank water for a long time. She
drank until her belly was full, waited a few minutes, and then drank
some more.

As soon as she hiked another half kilometer, she found another
road. This road wound through a more wooded area and it looked
green in the distance. Along the way, she found a barn that looked
abandoned. She slid through the squeaky wooden door into the shaded
building. Stacked along one wall, there were baskets of oranges. There

was a crate of figs. They were one of her favorite foods. She bit into the sweetness of a fig, and then peeled a couple of oranges. She ate so much that her stomach hurt. She cleaned up the peelings and climbed up to the loft of the barn. There in the soft hay, she curled up and slept. She slept all evening and through the night. In the morning she could hear the roosters crowing, and farmers outside talking. There were many women and men, helping to load a wagon full of the fruit. They were walking in and out of the barn. Marianna stayed hidden, because she was a fugitive, and not sure if it was safe to reveal that she was there. After a time she fell asleep again. She woke in the afternoon to a quiet barn. Looking around, she saw that everyone had left, along with all of the produce. She wished she had put some more figs in her pockets. At least she was alive and well fed.

Outside, once again, she walked down the road. It wound around down towards the sea. In the far horizon, there was a town. She did not recognize the town, nor the landscape. Again, the greenery turned to hard earth and lava rocks. These were ancient rocks, long ago formed from the volcano.

In the distance, she saw another vineyard in stark contrast to the black rocks before it. Then a farmhouse and several workers came into view. She stopped and spoke to the worker nearest the road, a woman, older than herself.

Can you help me? I am lost. What place is this?

The woman looked up and then quickly cast her eyes to the ground. She spoke quietly under her straw hat.

You need to hide quickly. Run and save yourself.

That is when she noticed a familiar figure moving towards her. It was Adolfo! How could it be? She had been running towards danger instead of away. Somehow, she had turned in the wrong direction. It was too late. He was after her again. This time she ran. On horseback, he was quickly in the road, blocking her way. She turned but her feet were much too sore to run anymore. Adolfo's whip caught her around the ankles and she went down into the dusty road. He dismounted and yanked her to her feet by her hair. The women kept their heads down and continued to work the field. Two more men rode up on horseback. Adolfo triumphantly shouted.

This is the bitch I told you about. She walked right back to me!

One of the men, clearly in charge commanded Adolfo.

Take her to the main house. She can start working after we have introduced her to Don Rimado.

Adolfo pushed her across the field. A sharp crack of his whip, stinging across her back and another on her shoulders hurried her pace.

DON RIMADO

D ON RIMADO WAS sitting in a room in front of a window that gave a grand view of the fields and vineyards far below. He was deep in thought with his hands clasped behind his head. It felt good to be back in Sicily again. It was different than the French countryside. Here, he could stretch out the farm in all directions and life was a slower pace. The death of his father, strangely gave him freedom, along with massive responsibilities. His wife Rosa loved it here as well. They had all they wanted from the land, and were friends with the Cosa Nostra. There were no problems to worry about. They were completely protected in this paradise. Don Rimado puffed on his cigar thinking about all of this. There was a knock on the big oak doors leading to his office.

Entre, sil vous plait

Rimado was an Italian by birth from Florence. His family moved to France when he was very young. He was bilingual and liked to flaunt this ability to Sicilians who he felt were beneath his station. His father was a *latifondisti* (absentee landlord) of the Etna Plantation. When his father died, he left the entire business to Rimado and his wife Rosabella. They decided to move from France and run the business in person. The business prospered until recently when blight attacked the orange and grape crops and rendered a heavy toll on his profits.

Just then—Adolfo shoved Maranna into the room.

Here is the woman I captured for you Don Rimado.

Marianna stood with head slumped down and her eyes to the floor. She was a wretched sight. Her body was racked with pain and her tool shed clothes were dirty and draped her like rags.

Don Rimado did not turn his chair around and continued to stare out the window. He spoke without turning.

Leave her here. You may go.

Adolfo was perturbed that he was so quickly dispatched. He knew his place and quickly left the room without comment.

Don Rimado thought that the idiot Adolfo was in a conflict with one of the workers again. He was more trouble than worth.

Don Rimado rose from his chair and walked around the desk. He scanned Marianna up and down and said nothing, continuing to puff on his cigar. Sitting back on the desk, he was visually upset and concerned.

Why are you dressed like this? Why do you have stains all over you and blood coming through the back of your shirt? Who are you?

Marianna.

Her answer was short and complete. She stated this without ego nor distain for this Don Rimado. She knew this man. Don Rimado stopped pacing as if stunned by something.

Marianna?

Don't you remember me? You took care of my husband Salvatore and I when were young. Adolfo had been beaten by my husband. Father Dominic and you—you Don Rimado yourself— you saved us.

Mon Dieu! Rosabella! Rosa!

He called for his wife. Rosa came into the room from the kitchen.

Rosa, would you please take this young lady, and clean her up. A hot bath would be good. See if we might have some clean clothes for her. And, also please give her a hot meal. She looks hungry. I shall meet with her later, after supper.

Rosa looked confused. She looked a little sideways at her husband.

Don Rimado quickly dispatched her.

Yes—yes—please do as I say. We will talk later as well.

Rosa turned to go. Just then as Rosa was leaving with Marianna, the two young and rugged men came through the door. These were the same two men Marianna had seen on horseback.

Ah, Marianna! Meet my two assistants, Raoul and Eduardo.

Marianna raised her eyes from the floor to acknowledge them. They both smiled and removed their hats. Marianna was confused as to why all of these men now acted like gentlemen.

Don Rimado, we have already had the pleasure.

Eduardo replied respectfully and bowed his head as did Raoul.

Rosa continued to rush Marianna out of the room and soon, just the three men were left. Don Rimado turned to Raoul.

Raoul, please close the door so the three of us may speak in private.

Please sit down my friends.

Don Rimado began to speak and the two men sat quietly and listened to his every word. Not often did they have these conversations with the Don.

So my stupid, stupid friend Adolfo brings this girl to us. Do you know who this girl is boys? She is the one and same wife of the man who died in the sulfur mine a few years ago. I gave very specific orders that she was to be left alone. We do not need her help here on this plantation. We have plenty of labor right now. Do you remember Salvatore? No, I don't think you were here then. Well, we worked him very hard and there was an accident. We did not kill this man on purpose. At that time, the policia in Palermo were sent out to investigate this accident. We were lucky to have friends in the right places. One thing we were to promise this policeman investigator and his friends, was that we were to leave this family alone. We gave them a good job on a friendly plantation with our friend Terzi. You remember Terzi. They have been working with excellent returns on their farm. Marianna and her sons have been making us money and they pay their fair share. They ask nothing from us and are good workers. This is how we pay them for their loyalty? Adolfo is a fool. He has gone against my commands before, but this is the worst thing that he could have done. All I can tell you is this-, protect this girl, Marianna, from him. I will do what I can to resolve this matter for everyone concerned. I do not want any more trouble. Her sons will come looking for her. I have heard that they are good boys and they love their mother and they will come here to find her. The younger boy is named Ben, and the older Sam. I do not want them harmed. Do you understand?

Both men nodded their heads. Don Rimado stared at them for a few minutes with a look that meant that this was serious business and a serious command. He was wondering if he could trust these men any longer. He had heard rumors, both from the workers, and his wife. He had heard that these men called him names behind his back. They had been talking within earshot of the workers and this undermined their confidence and respect for him. He was not sure about these men at all. He was sure that Adolfo was a fool.

THE CAVE

WHEN TUTU AND Ben arrived at the cave, they tied the horses in a small meadow, beyond the cave and down the hill. The horses were well hidden. They did not know how long they would have to wait until Sam would arrive. They expected at least a day and one half. They made themselves comfortable and found the supplies they always had stashed there. It was a cache of lanterns and ropes and camping things of that nature. They did not have extra food there because it would have spoiled anyway. Ben climbed up really high in the cave and Tutu wondered where he was going. He heard a shout from the top of the cavernous room.

It's here. We have wine my friend. This will help quench our thirst.

Tutu looked at Ben.

Tutu no drink wine.

Ben could not believe his ears. He thought that Tutu was joking with him.

Tutu! You have to drink this. It is pure and good for you.

Tutu no believe in alcohol. Allah say bad for you. Tutu no drink.

Ben thought to himself.

Suit yourself Holy man. More for me.

Night fall was coming and the cold rushed up the mountains. The temperature continued to drop and the boy and the man slept by the fire. Tutu got up several times during the night and stoked the fire. He seemed to sleep with one eye open. He looked up at the stars and wondered about his family. Soon, he would be home too.

Tutu thought to himself and stared up at the star filled skies.

Allah say, I help this boy. No matter what we find his momma. Tutu will do this for him. It is the will of Allah. If we have the will of his Jesus and my Allah, we can do anything—anything.

ROSABELLA

MARIANNA SAT WITH her back to Rosa and let the sudsy warm water roll down her back. Rosa was taking good care of her. This was strange for Marianna. One minute she was running from a crazy man and the next she was being treated like a princess. She did not understand the full meaning of Don Rimado's compassion. Rosa gave her a large towel to dry herself and then began to apply salve to the deep wounds on her back. She sighed with disgust that the man had treated her this way. Marianna asked her to explain what was happening. Rosa went through what she knew of her husband's kindness as well as the meanness of Adolfo.

One man can be so kind and the other so cruel. It seems that the one who has the power declines to use it unwisely, yet one who wishes this position is so quick to use unnecessary force. Adolfo has been jealous of my husband for a long time Marianna. I am happy that he doesn't run this plantation. He only works for us from time to time and he always abuses his power. Some men just wait for the chance to be wicked towards their fellow human beings.

He chased me like an animal! And—he uses that whip on me as if I were a horse.

If Don Rimado has anything to say about it, it will not happen again.

How can I be so sure?

My husband will give you a job inside the house for a few days with me. That way you can be of use, you can heal, and we can guard you against harm from Adolfo.

But I need to see my boys. My Sam—my Ben!!

In due time dear—In due time. Give my husband a chance to straighten this out. Now, rest for a couple hours. Then come downstairs and help me with dinner. It will just be you, me, and my husband. He wants to talk with you about everything.

Marianna was hoping that events were turning to better conditions for her. She wanted to be with her sons.

DINNER AND THE PLAN

D INNER WAS SERVED and a fine diner it was. Artichokes, grapes, olives, and ricotta cheese. That was just the appetizer menu. What followed was pasta with anchovies, plum tomatoes, and a light meat sauce, along with a fine table wine. Then almonds and canoli for dessert. Marianna had not seen such a feast. Rosa had the girls prepare the meal especially to set a better mood for her husband and Marianna.

When the meal was finished, Don Rimado, let Marianna sit and finish slowly anything else she might desire. He spoke softly to his audience of two.

In my business, it is not so easy to see those who might betray you at any time. This is such a time for us, here on this plantation. I don't feel a good trust from anyone. I know Sicilians trust no one, and I have learned from them. Still, it bothers me, when I treat everyone with such respect and receive so little in return. What I get—is envy—and jealousy from those who would cut my throat for my position.

But Don Rimado has respect for everyone regardless of their transgressions. It is how I have learned to rule our famiglia. And,

I have respect for you Marianna. My wife has respect for you too. She sees your pain as do I. I must tell you that your husband died in our sulfur mine many years ago, just north of here. The mine is abandoned now. At that time—

Don Rimado stopped for a moment because he saw that Marianna was becoming emotional. The final question of what happened to her husband was just answered. For all these years she had wondered—and wondered-

Ahem—ah—like I said—sorry Marianna—this happened as an accident. I know we worked him hard, but really this was an accident. We liked your husband—even though he was a slave in the mine—he was a good man. We respected him for his hard work, but many times he tried to escape. He almost succeeded the last time, but that was when he received—shall we say—an injury that he did not recover from. In his rush to escape, he fell many feet to his death in the mine shaft. No one could save him. This was the report from the men. It was investigated after our report, and we promised to take care of your family. That is how you came to know Terzi. It was not by accident as you think. Do you remember when you were introduced to Terzi by Vero in the marketplace. This was set up in advance. I know you are good friends with them now.

Lights and bells were going off in Marianna's head. Everything was becoming clear. She would slap Vero's face as soon as she could find him. Don Rimado, as if reading Marianna's mind-

I know you will be upset with Vero for not telling you all about this, but he was sworn to secrecy and he has truly fallen in love with your family. From time to time I have checked on him in the market. We know he does not pay all the protection money he should. We accept this even though we know he shorts us. We accept this because we know he takes care of you. We never wanted any trouble. We are not the bad Mafioso everybody paints us to be. Yes, we do not pay all the money we should to the field hands, but they survive and many would not have a job in these bad times.

He looked at Marianna for some time while she played with her food, thinking.

So, I am going to let you go.

Don Rimado said it just like that, in a matter of fact manner.

Marianna jumped up from her chair and hugged Don Rimado.

Thank you—thank you.

Don Rimado was surprised at her outburst of emotion. He laughed and said-

Now you must listen to me. I will send you with Raoul and Eduardo for safety reasons. They will escort you back to your home. I am also going to give you some money to take with you. It is for you and your boys. You must hide this money on you.

Marianna was in shock but accepted all of this with Don Rimado's good wishes. She hugged him again and thanked him.

My wife Rosa, will help you pack. You can leave first thing in the morning. I want to send some product to town anyway and you can ride the wagon with the men.

Don Rimado—I want to thank you for your honesty. Now I understand what I am to know about the past. I can't wait to talk with my boys.

It was finished and the plan was set. Rosa led Marianna off to pack.

THE MONEY

I T WAS LATE at night and Don Rimado was finishing up his
paperwork. He needed to remove some money from the safe
for Marianna. He also planned to have Eduardo and Raoul purchase
some goods at the market after they dropped off Mariana and sold the
products. He felt good about what he had done. He opened the safe and
then heard the gun click at his head.

What? What are you doing?

You are too soft old man.

It was Adolfo's voice. Raoul and Eduardo were with him as well.

You three are in together? Against me?

You are getting too old for this business—eh Don Rimado.
We can take some of this weight off of you now.

The men proceeded to gag Don Rimado and tie his hands and
feet. Raoul went in to Rosa's bedroom and hauled her out with a gag in her
mouth as well. They put her in the same small room off of the office.

Eduardo went into Marianna's room.

Come on girl. Don Rimado wants us to leave early. He said
we should leave before sun up and not to wake him nor his wife.
Hurry.

Marianna took this as fact. She did not suspect that Eduardo or Raoul were against Don Rimado. So she hurried and prepared her things for the trip. Marianna thought it was a bit odd but understood.

Can I just say good bye to Don Rimado and his wife?

No—no—no. We must not disturb them now. Let us go now!

Soon the two men were starting the wagon up the hill with Marianna in the back, sitting on some sacks of almonds. The men agreed that Adolfo would catch up later, so that Marianna would not suspect that something was wrong.

Don Rimado and Rosa were tied and gagged in the small room off of the office. No one heard their muffled cries for help.

The women field hands were all locked up in their small wooden huts with the doors barred from the outside. The men figured when they woke in the morning, they would have a big surprise waiting for them. No one would be there to unbar the doors.

The bandits now had two barrels of wine, two crates of figs, and Marianna sitting on the sacks of almonds. They also had a sack of silver coins from the Don. They left Rosa and Don Rimado to die. While Raoul and Eduardo drove the wagon, Adolfo choose a lower country road to travel and would join with them in the morning.

A SMALL ARMY

TUTU HEARD HIM first. It was Sam and Vero hiding the wagon and their horses. Tutu woke Ben.

Your brother is here early this morning.

All right then. We can get started. Can you fix us some coffee and breakfast?

Tutu not good cook. But—I make it for you now.

Tutu's coffee was so bad that the men spat most of it out. From now on Ben would make the coffee. The men broke some bread and ate it without anything on it. Time was important. Sam agreed that they should hurry and Vero and Ben agreed.

I did not expect you to come and help us, Vero. This is a surprise.

I figured you could use all the help you could get. Besides, I know exactly where to go. I know where she is.

All four contributed to the plan on how to find Marianna. They would move during the daylight until they were close to the plantation. Then they would move at night, quietly and swiftly. They would use the horses until they were close to the plantation, and then they would go forward on foot. Tutu took his machete, Ben his club, and Sam and Vero, nothing but their bare hands.

These four men were formidable, but they had no idea how many men or what they would face. Vero was positive of the destination because he was still familiar with Don Rimado. He wondered if Don Rimado had had a change of mind and captured Marianna himself. Vero had shipped many orders from the Don and his wife Rosa. This capture was still a mystery to him. He felt that something was odd about all of this. He was prepared to do what he could to bring Marianna back to the boys. He knew Sam could handle himself, but was concerned about young Ben. Then he remembered that Tutu would allow nothing to happen to Benedetto. He could think of no greater safety than the protection of Tutu.

SPYING

WHEN THEY FINALLY located the plantation and the big house they stopped for a moment and watched. From the trees, all they could survey was quiet. It was still dark and sunrise would not come for eight hours. They could see well enough in the moonlight to the huts near the field below the main house. Everything was still. They all moved down the hill toward the big house until they were within a few meters. Tutu was barefoot and said that he would go in and look around. None of the other three thought it was a good idea, but Tutu moved onto the veranda like a cat and then slid quickly inside. It was like he was a soft wind in the night. A few minutes later he walked outside like there was nothing wrong.

There is no one here but two people tied up. You want to untie them?

It is a man and a woman. Not young. No Marianna.

Ben, Vero, and Sam all looked at one another like they were lost in some dream.

Tutu was standing there, annoyed that no one was moving.

Are you coming?

Uh—yes—yes-

The three men stammered, finally joined Tutu, and walked in the front door of the house.

They untied Don Rimado and his wife Rosa. Don Rimado was excited that anyone even had found them. He quickly tried to explain everything but it was too confusing for the men.

Uh—robbed and then three men—and Marianna—his money—the buckboard—gone—her husband—Ben and Sam's father—

It all wound together like a ball of twine that could not be unraveled.

Finally Vero said,

All right—you are safe now—slow down and repeat it all— slowly!

After several minutes, more lamps were lit, and everyone sat at the dining room table. Don Rimado repeated the story, stopping along the way to make sure everyone understood. He was very careful to describe Adolfo, Raoul, and Eduardo. He described the direction he thought they might take the wagon because it was gone and so was Marianna. This would explain why they missed the wagon coming down to the house as they would have taken the road closer to the sea. So now, a new chase would begin. They realized that at least Adolfo was armed with a pistol. Since they thought there would be four against three, that there would be no problem.

Don Rimado requested that they return all three of the men to him at his home if they should catch them. The small posse left immediately on their mission.

THE RESCUE

WITHIN A MOONLIT nights ride, Ben and the men caught up with the thieves. They were sleeping around a campfire that had long burned out. Marianna was with them, but she did not know the whole story. She was sleeping in the back of the buckboard. She did not know that her escorts were really her captors, and she did not know that her sons were watching from the woods nearby. It would not be difficult for the two men to be captured. It took Vero some time to decide that they should attack. He was looking for the third man. They did not see Adolfo anywhere. Don Rimado said he was part of a gang of three. Why was he not with them? They decided to move in the early morning and take them by surprise. The two men never knew what hit them first, the club or the stone. But they were quickly beaten badly and tied up with plenty of rope. Vero and Sam loaded them in the buckboard. Rags were stuffed in their mouths to keep them quiet. The bags of money, two barrels of wine, and sacks of almonds were there as well. Tutu had his eyes on the woods. He decided to follow the buckboard, riding behind on Elsa.

Marianna was shocked by all of the commotion. It took her a few moments to understand who was who, and what was what.

Marianna hugged and kissed her sons like she had not seen them for years. She hugged and kissed Vero too but he blushed from the show of affection. Then she reached way up and hugged Tutu. This brought a huge smile to his face.

Pleased to meet you Miss Marianna.

The four men took the wagon and turned it towards Don Rimado's again. Tutu followed more than a hundred meters behind. Up front, on the buckboard, Ben explained everything to his mother. Vero and Sam rode lead on their two horses. Now at last, maybe everything was straight in her mind. She was beginning to wonder whether Adolfo was part of this plan.

Suddenly, out of the woods came a rider who jumped off his horse and held a pistol against the side of Marianna's head. Everything seemed to stop. The one with the pistol had the advantage here. Adolfo commanded Marianna to get down off the buckboard. He shoved Ben away and wrapped his arm around Marianna's neck. He squeezed her so tightly that the color ran from her face.

One move from anyone and I shoot her!

At that moment, nearly everyone was frozen in their actions. Tutu saw all of this happen in front of him. It happened so quickly, that everyone needed to adjust their senses. But Tutu knew what to do. Adolfo held his pistol high in the air, and made a big show of his surprise. Tutu rode like the wind and charged Elsa hard at Adolfo from behind. He held the machete tightly and sliced it through the air like a scythe. Adolfo turned when he heard the horse charging, it was too late. The black knight on the grey mount moved so quickly that no one noticed that Adolfo's hand and pistol were on the ground. With one swipe, Tutu had taken the machete and cut Adolfo's arm off at the wrist. He was cut so cleanly that even the victim had to look at his missing hand resting on the ground to realize what had happened. Then he screamed and let Marianna go. Blood spurted from his appendage and the boys were on him with ropes. Tutu tied Adolfo's feet together in the traditional fashion. But because Adolfo's wrist was hacked off, he used his machete to run another cut through Adolfo's upper arm, careful to cut only the muscle and not the bone or tendons. Through this opening, and through Adolfo's screams, he ran the rope and tied the arms together behind his back. Tutu did this in a nonchalant fashion, without emotion. That was when the screaming stopped and Adolfo passed out.

Now, all three of the robbers were tied up in the wagon. They turned back towards Don Rimado's home.

In the buckboard, Adolfo bled over the other two men, and all over the almonds.

DON RIMADO'S
BLESSINGS

DON RIMADO WAS sitting in front of his view window, and in the distance, on the other side of the vineyard, he could see them coming. He walked outside on the veranda, smoking a cigar, and enjoyed the sight of the entire procession coming back. Ben was driving the wagon with Marianna next to him. Vero and Sam led the group on horseback. Tutu followed from the rear, riding Elsa, with Ben's stallion in tow. The three evil men were roped, face down, among the sacks and barrels. Even at this advantage, Marianna still felt nervous. She kept looking back to make sure the men were tied securely. Don Rimado became jubilant and he offered all to go inside except Vero and Tutu. He walked around the wagon staring at the men. When Marianna, Ben, and Sam were inside his home, he quietly asked a favor of Vero and Tutu. Now, Don Rimado was stone-faced. His complete demeanor had changed.

Gentlemen, please take these men around back and down to my wine cellar. There is a dirt floor there. Toss them into the dirt. Do not untie them. Watch them and I will be down in a moment.

Oh, and Tutu, can you bring six of the empty barrels from the shed over there. Bring them down to the cellar for me as well.

Inside the house Rosa attended to everyone, bringing drinks and some baked goods she had made. Don Rimado walked through, greeted everyone and congratulated them on a job well done. He seemed so relaxed, yet resolute in his actions. He knew what he had to do. He walked the stairs down to the wine cellar and saw the men lying there on the ground. He told Tutu and Vero to go upstairs and have some refreshments with the others. He thanked Tutu for the empty barrels.

Tutu, would you be so kind as to leave me your machete? You can go now.

He arranged the men so they sat on chairs, Raoul and Eduardo on one side, and facing those two, Adolfo who was barely awake but aware of what was taking place. Don Rimado placed a hood over Raoul and Eduardo. He then threw a rope over the beam running across the eight foot cellar. He followed with a second rope in the same manner. After placing a noose around both men's necks, he stood them on chairs. He asked if there was anything they wanted to say but both men were silent and shaking. They knew what was next. Don Rimado reached up with his pistol and shot the first man in the head. His body kicked the chair out and he swung from the rafters. Then he followed exactly the same procedure with Raoul. Two men were dead, hanging from the rafters and Adolfo was watching frozen in fear. He had long since pissed his pants.

I did not give you a hood Adolfo, because I wanted you to watch the procedure and suffer as I have with you.

Adolfo struggled against his gag as if to say something.

Upstairs, the boys and Marianna all heard the shots. Tutu rose to go down, but Don Rimado's wife put her hand up as if to say, this is all right.

In the wine cellar Adolfo continued to struggle and then Don Rimado took out his gag rag.

Don Rimado took two of the barrels and placed them open ended under each man's body.

Adolfo felt he had to say something.

You can't fit those men's bodies into those barrels. They are way too big—you old fool.

Oh, you are right Adolfo. As always you are too smart for your own good. You can see that I have the three of you here. Can you not see that Adolfo?

Adolfo was silent in response as Don Rimado brought forth the machete.

You see, I have six barrels here to handle the situation. Can you do the mathematics in your head Adolfo?

As he said that, he began to slice through Raoul's body, just below the ribcage. While he was slicing, he counted out loud.

One half and one half make one. No? Then—one half and one half make one again. That's four halves, and that makes—uh—two!

Now we have a problem eh Adolfo? We have one person left and two barrels. Oh—I know now. One half and one half—it makes one again!

When all that connected the upper and lower halves of the body was a bony skeleton piece, he swung the machete hard through the spine. The legs fell into the barrel. Don Rimado turned to see the horror on Adolfo's face. He returned the gag to Adolfo's mouth because only Don Rimado could visualize what would happen next. He repeated the procedure on Eduardo's body and then put the upper parts of each into the next two barrels. He now had four barrels full of half men. Blood was all over the dirt floor of the cellar. He then turned to Adolfo.

Now Adolfo, we will take care of you. We have to finish the mathematics no? I have saved you for last because you revile me so. This makes me sad that I must do the same with you.

However, I must say that there is one small difference here Adolfo. I will not shoot you <u>before</u> I cut you in half. I do not want to waste another bullet on you.

Adolfo rolled off the chair, screaming in horror through his gag, as the Don put the rope around his neck. The screams could be heard through the rags and all throughout the house. After all was finished, he dug some of the cellar dirt and filled the remainder of the barrels, leaving some space.

He called upstairs for Vero and Tutu to come down and help him. They walked down the stairs but were only shocked to see the amount of blood covering Don Rimado. He asked them to use the wheel barrow and go outside to a pile of small rocks and please bring some in.

They helped fill the remainder of the barrels with rocks and helped the Don seal them closed. When they were done, Don Rimado excused himself to take a bath. He told the men to clean up as well and plan to spend the night.

His wife prepared a wonderful meal and the Don toasted all of them as heroes.

The next morning, the Don welcomed everyone to breakfast. After the breakfast, he invited them all into his office. You would never know of the horror of the night before. It was just business as usual. The Don spoke.

Gentlemen, and young lady, Marianna too—In Sicily, justice is swift. We save money because we are the police force, the judge, the jury, and the executioner—all in one. It is a waste of time to talk about it. It's almost like the Pope and excommunication. We must keep the order and the respect for the famiglia. This is Cosa Nostra.

He made the sign of the cross and he moved one arm up to the ceiling and then the other across left to right, very deliberately.

It's a this—away and a this—away. And—your problems go away.

We save time and effort for everybody. Let me ask all of you—don't you feel better this morning? What's the matter? I don't see anyone smiling. Come on. Let's have some café and some fried dough from my wife. It tastes so good this morning. Bon Giorno.

Everyone was silent and wide-eyed.

On the desk were five neat piles of gold coins and silver coins. He designated one pile to each. Marianna was first and he gave each of them a bag in which to put their money. Tutu and Vero were next with one bag each, followed by the brothers. They were all stunned.

I feel that I must share all of this with you. You have saved our lives and our fortune. In return for this, I have given those of you who need to know, my last instructions. Vero, you and I have another matter to discuss as well. If that is all, you best be on your way home. Maybe our paths will cross sometime. Until then I bid you Adieu, mes amies.

When they returned outside, the buckboard was loaded with goods, fresh bags of almonds to replace the blood-soaked ones, cartons of grapes, and the six barrels. Vero took the reins and all were off towards home.

PLANS FOR A NEW LIFE

WHEN ALL FIVE of the group landed at Terzi's farm, he and his wife came out to greet them. They could not believe that everyone was alive and well. Vero lifted a bag of almonds from the wagon and gave them to Terzi.

This is for you old man.

Take it up to the house for me please.

You will have to carry it yourself. Work some of that fat off.

Terzi was taken back.

Vero continued.

We are all free men and women now, but we will treat you well if you are civil to us.

Terzi was still confused as well as his wife, Anna.

I will explain it all to you in time my friend.

Vero slapped him on the back as he said this.

What are you going to do with all of that wine on the cart?

Terzi was curious.

Oh, all of this is to be shipped out. I have my orders from Don Rimado.

Don Rimado? You have been there?

Yes, he said to send his good wishes to you and your wife. Uh, we need to be going now.

As he said this, Vero and Tutu, pulled away, leaving the two boys and their mother to themselves at the cottage.

As they rode into the sunset on the buckboard, Vero turned to Tutu and said,

I didn't know you were so handy with a machete.

Tutu looked at him and responded.

Yes, Tutu use something like machete in Africa, but bigger. I no use it like Don Rimado.

They both laughed at the cruel joke. Vero wanted to continue the conversation.

I will have you off to see your family on your island within a couple of days. I have some small things to do at the shop first. I hope you don't mind working for me for your passage.

What Vero did not tell Tutu, was that he had a surprise for him. It would take him a couple of days to prepare the surprise, but he knew Tutu would like it. The two bantered back and forth, Vero in his fluent Sicilian dialect, and Tutu in whatever dialect he was using at the time. They had developed a bond that was as strong as any in the Sicilian world. Vero was in a talkative mood.

Tutu spoke up.

Tutu must pray. Vero need to be quiet now.

Vero didn't say a word for the rest of the trip.

The next day Vero called on a couple of his local contacts to make arrangements for a passage to New York for Sam and his mother. Ben was going to stay for a time to work for Vero. The tickets for the Mendoza needed to be ordered. It was a large steamship that would take sixteen days to reach Ellis Island. Vero called upon every favor he had earned over the years. He wanted to make the trip comfortable for Marianna and Sam. Vero made sure that they had sleeping quarters. He also was certain to provide extra food that they might take with them.

Vero was a busy man. At the direction of Don Rimado, he purchased the steamship tickets several weeks in advance. He also spent several days down at the docks with a boat builder named Grimaldo. They had many arguments over specifications and money issues. When it was nearly done, Vero visited the craftsman one more time. They decided what the name of the vessel would be, and some last minute details were discussed. Grimaldo was surprised that Vero had so much money to spend on such fine matters as mast rings and so forth. Vero spared no expense. Every time that Vero returned to his shop and the time drew nearer for departure, he grew more depressed. He was not going to see his beloved Marianna and Sam much longer. Therefore, he busied himself with every detail of the preparations.

Marianna will have a voyage to remember. I must not let Don Rimado think that I did a poor job.

READY TO SAIL

VERO WANTED TO make sure that he was following Don
Rimado's instructions to the letter. He read the note
several times to make sure. It was the day of departure and everything
at the dock was ready. Vero had timed it perfectly. Marianna and
Sam were in the shop with all of the baggage tied together and it was
ready for the cart. First the cart had to be unloaded. It contained six
barrels that everyone was familiar with plus two extra barrels that were
identical. Vero announced that everyone should walk down to the pier
and Sam would drive the wagon with Marianna in the front seat. Tutu
would follow behind and help with the loading.

Before them loomed a fifteen meter craft, that was gleaming
in the sun. Her bow rose some two meters above the water line, and
she sat in the water as if she owned the sea. Upon closer inspection all
could see that she was spotless. A group of sailors were standing on the
dock admiring the craftsmanship of Grimaldo. The lines were coiled
perfectly on the spotless decks to show her in all her glory. Even the
scuppers were sanded and smoothed to perfection. Her construction
showed that she could be fast as well as functional. Great care was taken
to have a keel that could handle the size of the mast and sail. A smaller

jib was attached to the bow. Everywhere the wood shined as if covered in a glass coating. Tutu stood looking at the craft, wondering whose boat this was. He turned to Vero and asked.

Is *this your new boat?*

No-no Tutu. *This boat belongs to a Very rich Tunisian.*

Tutu looked at Vero and Sam, perplexed.

Finally Ben yelled out.

It's yours Tutu!!!

Tutu walked slowly towards the boat and ran his hand up and down the gunwale. Then he walked towards the bow and stared at the lettering.

It said-

Il Tonno Grande

He turned around and looked at the group and started laughing. With tears in his eyes, he hugged every one of them.

Vero spoke up.

If we don't get this loaded soon we are all going to be late and in trouble.

All pitched in to help load, even Marianna. She helped carry several small packages they had prepared for Tutu. The eight barrels were lined up in the hold, just above the keel. The boat handled the weight easily. Ben helped load the boat with other supplies such as extra flour, sugar, and almonds. Everything was set to go. Ben leaped in the boat with Tutu.

Tutu was surprised.

Where are you going young Ben?

I am going with you. You said I could visit anytime. No better time than now. Besides, someone needs to help you steer around the rocks out there.

The whole group had a hearty laugh on that. Just then, an inspector walked on the dock. Recognizing Vero, he asked him if the boat was in proper order.

I don't own the boat. It belongs to my friend Tutu—over there.

You don't mind if I check some of the cargo—do you?

Vero started to sweat a little.

No—no go ahead.

Vero hoped that the inspection would be cursory and uneventful.

The inspector turned to Tutu and Ben, and said-

Bring a barrel of that wine up here and let me look at it please. Let me have that second one from the end.

The second one from the end just happened to contain Adolfo's lower parts. The barrels were marked, but hopefully the inspector did not notice these small markings.

Vero sprang into action.

I'll help him with that Inspector. Marianna, would you please give the information on the departure to the inspector please.

As if on cue, Marianna knew exactly what to do. She turned on every feminine charm she had. She sidled up to the inspector and got his eyes turned away for just a moment. In the meantime, Tutu grabbed a barrel single handedly and switched it to second from the end. Tutu knew wine from swine. When the inspector turned to look again, He and Ben were lifting the barrel to the dock from the second place. The inspector took a wine barrel tool and opened the bunghole. He siphoned a small bit a wine into a flask. Looking at the wine and then swishing it around carefully, he lifted it to his nose. All was quiet on the dock. He put his lips to the flask and sipped. It was still quiet. He took his notebook and scribbled something. He made a stern face and faced Vero, the dockmaster.

Did you sell this to this man?

Why yes—yes I did!

Vero looked worried.

I hope you paid a high price for this—it is excellent!

He turned and walked away, pronouncing his departure.

Arrivederci!

Ben quietly stated to Vero.

Good thing you have this dock covered Vero. If you didn't have these guys paid off we might have been in jail.

Vero looked at Ben and raised his eyebrows.

Never saw the man before in my life.

Let's get out of here.

Ben and Tutu waved as they pushed away from the dock. Tutu raised the small sail and Ben ran around like he knew what he was doing. Then, he manned the oars.

Marianna, Vero, and Sam hurried back to the shop with the empty wagon. They had to unload and catch the small boat that would take them to a larger port, before embarking on the Mendoza, a large steamship.

On the dock, Marianna and Vero embraced for a long time. Finally, Sam broke the mood and asked where the passage tickets were. Then Vero spoke-

Maybe when Ben comes to New York, I will come with him. The way business is going around here, it will be a good change. The three laughed, hugged, shook hands, and tried to seem cool about it all, but it was not possible. Extreme emotions welled to the surface, and when the boat pulled away, Vero, stood there as a lost soldier, waving good bye.

A voyage that would take over two weeks took them to Ellis Island, NY. That is where many of the immigrants would enter the United States of America. They would pass the Statue of Liberty and experience the wonder and joy, and excitement of a new life. They did not know what the future held for them, they only knew what they left behind. They would bring their every part of their culture embedded within them.

Many from Sicily emigrated to different parts of the Americas, either to New Orleans, or Argentina. Wherever they landed, they changed the world.

IL TONNO GRANDE

Il Tonno Grande turned from the harbor and straight out of the cut. She pointed her bow as if she were driving for the North African coast. A soft east wind filled her massive main nicely. The sun was out and the water was a clear blue green that one only sees in southern waters. Ben stood in the bow and held his arms to the sky. He let the spray wash over him. He looked down and saw the dolphin racing along the side and ahead as if to lead the way. They rejoiced in spinning and playfully leaping through the spray.

Tutu was at the tiller and had the main sail sheet chocked as usual. This time, the ride was faster and smoother. He sailed right past his home in Favignana, knowing he would be returning soon. He could see the island in the distance off the port side. He longed for home and would have adventuresome tales to tell his wife. Some of the mission was sworn to secrecy with Don Rimado and Vero. He would keep the faith. Tutu always kept his word. With the gold, silver, and the priceless boat he was piloting, he was a rich man. He knew he was rich even before this adventure, but it would be nice to be more comfortable. His mission was almost finished.

Ben would be his friend forever. Without Ben saving his life, none of this would have happened. Tutu thought about many things as he steered towards the center of the Mediterranean Sea. He thought about the way lives cross paths. He thought about Allah and he thought about Jesus. He thought about all religion and what it meant. He thought that loving your fellow man was the most important rule of all. Was that what all religion taught you?

He realized that the wind had died down. The sea was almost calm. It gave one an eerie feeling when no land was in sight in any direction, yet the water all around you was like glass. Ben and Tutu looked at one another and shrugged shoulders alike. Ben spoke up.

I guess this is as good a place as any.

Yes, Let us do this now.

Ben and Tutu wrestled each barrel to the proper position and pushed them overboard. They both leaned over the side to watch each barrel sink, trying to see it as long as they could. They sank until the light could not illuminate them any longer. There were two barrels left on the deck.

Both men knelt on the deck, each to their own thoughts. One put his forehead on the deck, and the other made the sign of the cross. After a few moments, each turned, waiting for the next hint of wind.

Soon, the afternoon breeze picked up, and the main began to fill. Tutu let Ben handle the tiller, and he moved forward to adjust the sails. The boat leaped for joy and turned toward Favignana. Tutu spoke first.

My wife will be pleased to meet such a young man as you Ben. I am afraid my daughters will find you too handsome as well. Maybe we should take you back to Vero.

Tutu was laughing as he said this. But in humor there is always a hint of truth. Tutu had two beautiful young women for daughters, and they always wore a scarf around strangers. Ben would be staying for some time so there needed to be some discussion between Tutu and Ben.

You know you can trust me Tutu. I am hurt that you think this of me. You know that I am a virgin don't you.

It is not you who I am worried about. My two daughters, Amira and Palika are sixteen and ten. Amira is in the flower of her youth. She is a beautiful young woman and I know she desires to find a man. She has discussed this many times with her mother. Mira has tried to tell her to be patient and the right young man will find her. She is not so sure. When I bring you home, she will think that you are the one, my handsome young Ben.

Ben laughed and thanked Tutu for the complement.

Tutu continued.

I want you to know that I consider you a great young man. I respect you. I would gladly give my daughters hand in marriage to you. However, I do not want her deflowered if that is the only thing both of you desire. I think you have more control of this than my young Amira. That is all I will say about this matter to you, my friend. There is nothing on earth that will ruin our friendship.

Ben felt overwhelmed by this outpouring of Tutu's feelings about such delicate matters. He was frankly, a little embarrassed by all of it.

He wanted to change subjects.

Tutu. Do you think we can catch some big tuna?

Next month, when they start running. Our backs will be sore from pulling them in. You will become a man Ben.

As he said this they pulled into Favignana harbor. Ben helped with the lines as Tutu took the helm. After the Big Tuna was docked, they carried several items to the dock. The barrels of wine they bartered right there for flour and sugar. Ben forgot that Tutu did not drink, nor did anyone in his family. Several dock handlers showed up to help and Tutu was greeted with a big homecoming cheer from his friends. One of the men remarked that they thought he was lost at sea. They had not talked with his wife. Tutu told them that he had found a little brother in Ben and brought him home with him. After that, all kinds of joking and other business matters, were handled. No one knew of Tutu's new riches, but they remarked about his handsome new boat, Il Tonno Grande. Tutu passed it off and said that now he owed a great deal of money to several people. Tutu told Ben to stay and watch the boat, while he walked to his home and brought back the wagon.

Ben leaned back on the stern of the boat and acted like he owned it. Many sailors came by and looked at him as if he were a young rich man. In many ways he was.

THE ISLAND HOME

IT SEEMED LIKE he was waiting forever. Finally he saw Tutu leading a mule pulling a cart. The cart was painted many colors, and the mule wore a colorful harness. Tutu pulled the cart out onto the pier right next to the boat.

All right Ben. We can load it up. My wife Mira will be cooking a dinner that you will not forget. That is what took me so long. I had to embrace my wife and daughters. I have told them all about you. You had better protect yourself Ben. They will feel very obligated to you for saving my life.

I told you to stop that. I only did what anyone would do.

Well, we shall see my friend. We shall see what happens next.

All of this time Tutu was smiling and working. He had a permanent grin on his face. He was happy to be home. Ben felt like a vagabond. His brother and mother were gone to another world, and his father had passed on to the next. He was deep in thought when Tutu jabbed him in the ribs.

Let us go to Tutu home—Tutu hungry. I know Ben hungry.

He poked Ben in the gut.

The road to the house was rocky and rutted. The mule kept the steady pace and Ben and Tutu were bounced around on the buckboard. They looked so incongruous—The great big black African man next to the thinner younger Sicilian boy. Towards the west, you could see the sun beginning to set on the horizon. The waves were calming again. It was as peaceful scene as one could imagine as if inside a painting. Ben spoke first as they jostled along.

I can see why you like it here.
Tutu love it here.
It is so much like an island.
It is an island.
There are many sea gulls.
Yes, there are many birds.
You are in paradise.
I am in paradise. You like Vero—talk—talk—talk—Ben be quiet—Tutu pray now.

Ben laughed to himself and he shut his mouth. The only noise heard was the wagon in the ruts and the clip—clop of the mule's hooves.

VERO'S SHOP

Vero knew Ben would be back in a few weeks. But Vero knew it would be a long time before he would see Sam or Marianna. He might never see them again. He was sad and happy at the same time. He was happy that his friends escaped this Sicilian paradise before it exploded. He heard rumblings of war-war between nations and war between families. He heard these things because of his position on the wharf and his place among the traders. He took a day off from work and rode out to Terzi's house. He asked if he might keep up the little cottage down in the field and Terzi obliged him to do so. When Ben came back, maybe they could do something on the farm and sell product on the docks. He didn't know. He was just thinking. He spent some time cleaning up the place and surveying the farm. The horses were fed well enough, but he paid them a visit anyway. Vero was now a lonely man. As he was sweeping the floor in the cottage, he found a note on the table addressed to Ben. Ben must have forgotten it, or maybe Marianna intended for him to find it after she left. Vero thought for a moment. He knew that Ben could not read and Marianna knew that as well. She must have intended for someone, anyone really, to read it to Ben. It might as well be Vero. He opened the folded paper. It was not sealed.

To my dearest Son Ben—I know you will find this long after I am gone to America. I want you to follow Sam and me as soon as you can. You are young yet, and I wish you to enjoy your youth. Sicily will soon be a bad place to live and you must come as soon as you are able. Vero will watch over you and you must help him too. I know you will spend time with Tutu. As you are the youngest, your father used to say that I must protect you all that I can. Well, now you see that I am not close enough to do that anymore. Maybe Vero will come with you to America. I suspect that his business will be declining soon, just as so many others are. There are hungry people everywhere in Sicily. No one knows who to trust. Hungry people can be dangerous. Please be careful and soon, we will write to you from our new home in America. We wait for you as soon as you are able to come. Your loving mother, Marianna

Vero was moved by the note and he knew he must read it to Ben as soon as possible. Riding back to the shop at the wharf, Vero thought of everything that had happened. They had been to the Devil and back and they were all healthy and well, except for Salvatore. He thought about what an incredible human being Salvatore was. He left that legacy with his sons. Vero was proud that he had helped. He might even go to church this Sunday.

FAVIGNANA

Each day Ben and Tutu would sail out of the harbor just before sunrise. They would fish all morning and be back in the harbor in the early afternoon. After trading and tidying up the boat, they went to Tutu's house and worked in the garden or helped milk the goats. After a short bath and nap, they all showed up at evening meal. Tutu and Mira would sit at one end of the table. The girls Amira and Palika sat on each side of the table. Mira rarely sat at the table, but continually served and filled drinks. Tutu asked her to sit and everyone was quiet for a moment. Tutu went into an explanation that Ben was like family and that his daughters and wife no longer needed to wear their kerchiefs around him. It was all right to be comfortable in their own home. The women were surprised. Ben felt humbled. So now was the moment Ben would see Amira's hair fall down around her shoulders and all of her beauty from under the head covering. His eyes nearly popped out of his head. Amira's almond eyes and perfect brown skin accentuated her entire face. Ben could not stop staring so he purposely put his head down and looked at his plate. Tutu was surprised at Ben's reaction and asked what was wrong.

Nothing is wrong! That is the problem.

It is all right Ben. I have given my permission.

Your women are all so beautiful that I have no words for this.

The girls laughed at him and his embarrassment. Bens face was red.

Ben excused himself and went outside. Tutu looked at Mira and asked her to go out and speak with Ben.

Isn't that your position to do this my husband?

I give you my permission woman. Now go to him.

Mira did not know what to think so she obeyed. She did not put her shawl back on nor cover her face. Ben was staring into the starry night sky, lighting up a shimmering bay, more than a kilometer away.

Ben. Ben.

Ben did not turn to face her.

Ben. Look at me.

Again, Ben was stunned by her beauty.

I do not know how to act—or what to say. I feel like a child.

She put her hands on Ben's shoulders and stared straight into his eyes.

Ben. You are no longer a child. My husband knows this. You are not experienced in love and these matters. That is the way it should be.

My daughters are not laughing at you Ben. They are laughing because they are nervous too. This is the first time they have shown their faces to another man other than their father. It is against our way. We have difficulty with this too. Can you understand?

Uh—yes. I think so.

If you are to live here with us for such a long time, we need you to be part of our family. This way we can live at ease with one another's hearts. My husband has told me all about you for many hours. I know who you are Ben. You are a good man. You are not a child any longer. As a young man you have many desires for women. This is not a bad thing. This is a good thing that you have this need for love. Now, you must control this until it is the proper time. We have had many conversations with our daughter Amira. Palika is too young.

Please come back in to the table and join us for the rest of dinner.

She took Ben's arm and walked him back in as if she were his escort.

Ben sat at the table sheepishly. Tutu was happy that his wife completed her little mission and dinner continued on. Tutu spoke up next.

Tomorrow we no go fishing. I have a building project for you Ben. We are going to work on the barn, where you have been sleeping. We will make it better.

The next morning everyone was up early and all were assembled in front of the barn. They woke up Ben and they laughed at him as he was summoned to begin work. Tutu handed Ben a crowbar and pointed to some boards.

Those boards over there need to come off. We are going to extend that part of the barn.

Soon everyone was working and Ben liked the feeling of being a carpenter without any knowledge of what he was doing. The girls were carrying away the boards. Often Amira would brush Ben when grabbing a board. Ben looked at her and she would smile a smile that went through Ben. Amira was playing with him. He knew this and was able to return the favor, often touching her when handing a board to her. It was getting too hot on the Island of Favignana for this cavorting. Tutu saved the day by ordering the girls off to milk the goats. He admired Ben's handiwork and patted him on the back.

Nice work Ben. Now we will sink a couple of posts over here.
Then tomorrow we will close it all up and you will have extra room.

Tutu knew exactly what he was doing in construction and all other matters.

That night, as Ben lay up in the loft bed of the barn, he could see straight into Amira's bedroom window. She did not douse the lamplight as she undressed in front of the window. At first Ben did not look away from all of her beauty, and then he rolled over and went to sleep. The next day Ben and everyone finished the barn project and Ben asked Tutu if, in a few days, he might give him a boat ride back to Vero's wharf. He said he missed Vero and needed to check on his cottage. Tutu understood, and after the construction was completed, he said good bye to everyone they walked down to the harbor. Amira was crying and ran after Ben. She threw her arms around him and said that she didn't want him to go. Amira's parents did not interfere with this, but rather obliged them their private moment. Soon afterward, Ben caught up with Tutu and thanked him for his hospitality. Tutu understood all of it, as usual. When they got to the dock in Trapani, Vero was waiting. Before departing, Tutu gave Ben a grand embrace befitting true friendship among men.

Tutu honored you come anytime. Visit me and my family on Favignana.

Maybe someday Tutu. Maybe someday. You take care and be careful with your new boat. I want to pull the tuna in the nets Tutu. So, in a month, I will come and see you again.

It was difficult for Ben, but he had to walk away from one of the best friends of his life, for a little time. Because Tutu's daughter was too beautiful to behold, it was best to let things cool down for a few weeks.

THE COTTAGE

VERO WELCOMED BEN back and they had a good talk about everything that had happened since the departure of Ben's family. They talked into the night hours and Ben stayed with Vero for the next two days.

Vero told Ben that he had been keeping up the cottage and Ben rode out to see Terzi and his wife. Terzi said he was desperate for some help and offered to pay Ben handsomely for his work. Ben accepted and said that he needed to help Vero at least three days a week as well. They worked it all out and soon Ben was plowing Terzi's fields with the mule.

Ben did not hear from Tutu for the next three weeks, or the beautiful Amira. It was better this way. Ben was afraid of offending the entire family.

One morning, Ben thought that it was time and hitched a ride through Vero's influence, over to Favignana. Tutu was surprised and delighted to see Ben at the dock, waiting for him. They went out and pulled the nets for Tuna. Every day, Ben's back was sore. He slept out in the newly constructed barn. Amira was no longer a problem. She had found a good Muslim man on the island and fallen in love with him. Her father was happy and so was Ben. Living with Tutu's family became easier. After two months of work, Ben went back home to the cottage. He had earned a nice sum of money.

On more than one occasion Ben had visits from the local farmers. He shared stories of Tuna fishing with them. He started to develop many friends with neighbors. Sometimes he met young girls at the feasts in town. He became a young man about town and for the next five years he saved for his trip to America. He lost his virginity along the way, with a young lady from town. He didn't know if it made him more of a man. What he did know was that it did not end the work, either on the farm, or on the docks with Vero. He learned to relax around women after his experiences with them. He did not show off or try to be a lady's man, although he did have a lady friend in town make some new clothes for him.

At first he went to church more often on Sundays. That held his interests for a few months and then he did not go again. It wasn't about religion; it was that he did not like the political atmosphere of the church. After mass, many of the women of the congregation were introducing him to their daughters. They had ideas of marriage. Ben was not ready for that and politely told them so, but they would not take no for an answer. This was the way he survived on his own. He would travel into town because he was lonely. He would get his fill of people and strangers. Then, he wanted to be alone again. In this time he taught himself how to cook. He was becoming a very good chef. His menu was full of variety, and he enjoyed trying new things. He tried baking bread with olives in the dough. He tried that same recipe with sausage in the bread. He added different types of cheese into the menu. He liked all kinds of wine. Terzi was a **Gabelloti**. But most **Gabelloti** were hated by the locals. Terzi was different. He liked Ben, and besides, Ben had earned his own way now. He still helped Terzi run the farm for his rent, but otherwise, Ben's life was his own. It was rare to find a Sicilian that controlled his own life at that time.

Terzi had a guitar and allowed Ben to try it. He took some lessons from Terzi's niece and he became fond of her. He learned to sing some traditional Italian folk tunes. She taught him guitar, and he taught her to cook. They had fun together, but again, Ben faded away from a relationship, because he liked his introverted life style too much.

Ben liked to be up in the mountain passes and often took Elsa for overnight camping expeditions. He was a bachelor in paradise. The thing that held back Ben the most, was his failure to learn to read. He had little schooling beyond the second grade because of the events in his life. He had to work for the family and help his mother when he was young. Ben was great with numbers, and could do large computations in his head. The failure to read and ability to do mathematics caused him to turn in certain directions later in his life.

When Ben went into town, he met many street children that were turning to crime in order to feed themselves. He caught one pick pocketing on him. After a short conversation, he gave the child, a small amount of money to buy something to eat. Together with Vero, they began to feed many, many children. Ben felt good about this charity, even though neither he nor Vero would be considered rich by any standards.

He wondered about his brother Sam, and what kind of work he found in America. He heard through Vero, that his brother was a foreman on the New York Railroad line. He hoped to hear more from him and his mother soon. Ben was feeling melancholy one evening, while camping. He sat next to the campfire and talked to his most faithful companion, Elsa.

Well, big girl, this is how we live now. We are like vagabonds, you and me. I wonder if you can stand a few more years with me Elsa? Will you be my friend for all that time? I will always be your pal Elsa. Ben will always have the sugar and bread for you. You have never failed me. Do you think I will find the right girl sometime? Maybe in America. Eh? No, I will not take you with me Elsa. You cannot go across the big water. Your place is in Sicily. I would like to live in Sicily the rest of my life. I love it here. But now, Sicily is going to have big problems. Many do not have enough food to eat. I hear rumors of more war among peoples I do not know.

We will wait for Sam to send me notice to come to America. Then we shall see. Tomorrow, maybe we will ride out to see Vero. Then, maybe, Vero and I could take a ride to see Don Rimado. I sense that many Sicilians are having less and less to eat. Everyone seems poor. I think you will like a nice long ride Elsa. I know you have a free spirit like mine.

In the next few days, Ben talked with Vero and Don Rimado. Things were not going that well for either of them. Ben heard of political organizations that were not friendly to either Vero or the Don. Things were moving from bad to worse for Sicilians. They began to plan a move. All three of them began to dream of a new future in America.

Ben thought of the future

I must leave my beautiful Sicily.

AUTHORS COMMENT:

John Eldredge in **Wild at Heart**, quotes Bly as saying, Not receiving any blessing from your father is an injury . . . Not seeing your father when you are small, never being with him, having a remote father, an absent father, a workaholic father, is an injury.

I am indebted to the many fine authors who have written about the Sicilian experience. This story is about eighty per cent verifiable. Some characters and situations have been added for effect. Some names have been changed or used with different characters to protect the privacy of those individuals. The basic plot of the story is true. My grandfather told me of these events many times. Unfortunately, I did not learn to speak Italian very well. I was able to understand most of what my grandfather told me in broken English. I was able to check out many of the facts through the internet and also from the work my son Thomas did on ancestry.com. Actually, my oldest son was able to have some time with his great grandfather before gramps passed on. I was fortunate to be able to have my grandfather on this earth into my thirties. The fact that my grandfather lost his father very young is a tragedy that faced many Sicilian youths. His route to America, through Ellis Island, is one that thousands of immigrants experienced. The fact that he followed his brother, only further emphasizes the fact that everyone who could get out of Sicily, emigrated as quickly as possible. The conditions of poverty, famine, and slavery were real for millions.

Eventually, after coming to America, my grandfather would feed many people during the depression. His good-hearted nature endeared him to many of the local town people. He turned his grocery store into a restaurant and a bar. His ability to cook enabled him to feed many at a low cost. Instead of bread lines, he allowed people to come into the restaurant and eat for free. He always said to people, you can pay me later when you have money. Some did but I don't want to give away the next story in America. I want you to read my next book. I want you to read about the rest of the life of "Mr. Benny". Mr. Benny is the affectionate name given to my grandfather after he started his businesses in the USA. He was a very kind and compassionate soul. He has always encouraged me to *"give"* until it hurts, to help other people. I believe that this is the true nature of being *"religious"*. I don't ever remember my grandfather going to mass on Sunday, but rather, I remember him being a helpful soul to others, *every day*.

I am not writing this story to state that my grandparents were any different than many of the immigrants that came to America. We don't hold any special privilege. I have written it to illustrate where we have been as Sicilian-Americans and why we are the way we are. My grandparents would want to be called Americans and not the hyphenated version. My father, Jack Dominic, fought in WWII. They were all so proud to be American. History further illuminates what too many of us forget, that life was just flat out "tough", and people did what they had to do to make it. There was no use complaining about your position in life. You had to change it or die trying. Another reason for writing in a creative non-fiction format, is to put myself outside the story, to better describe what everyone was feeling and experiencing inside Sicily at that time. I did not want my own ego to get in the way.

I suppose if you are an Irish-American, Polish-American, or African-American immigrant, your story is exciting to write as well. I encourage you to write it so that we all might read it. I feel that there is an inverse correlation between intelligence and prejudice. The more intelligent you are, the less likely you will be to have a prejudiced view of other people. By intelligent, I don't mean how much school you have had, or how many degrees you have earned. I mean a real world intelligence, where you read a great deal, whether it be the internet, newspapers, or magazines. If you travel, you will find interesting people wherever you go. It can enrich your life. My visit to Sicily was brief, but I intend to go again.

I wanted to create a *feeling* for what was happening at that time. I hope you enjoyed the story as much as I enjoyed writing it, and I hope you would comment on the book either to me personally, or on the net. I tried to write it in a very simple style, much as my grandfather would relate to me. You will not find very long sentences, nor difficult to understand verbosity. This was intentional.

I did not intend to degrade or vilify any religion or race in writing this story. If you were offended, please accept my apology. There is no desire to portray women as being less important than men. If my great-grandmother did not survive all of her trials, I would not be here writing this story. As far as direct influence in everyday life, the men were much more influential. Because this was true in my family, does not mean it is true for everyone's family, of course. Men, whether they were relatives, school teachers, or coaches, served to play an important role in my life.

This is my first attempt at writing anything as long as this story, so I expect that there will be both negative and positive comments. Keep it clean and take it easy. I have an ego that can get bruised like anyone else. I have a young spirit, but I am growing old too quickly. Sometimes I get crabby. I try to put forward my good natured qualities, but often the emotional nature of an ancient Sicilian will come pouring out.

If the good Lord is willing, I will write parts II and III, continuing in America for our family. As the story is more recent, it will become more factual as a percentage of work.

I realize that this first book is rather short. It is only an introduction to the background of our family, and especially, Mr. Benny. The following two sections of Father- Father- Father will be considerably longer. I wanted to get my bearings as to how to best approach the whole process. Please forgive me if you felt it was too short. As I retire from my professor position, I will have much more time to write.

I am indebted to Philip Gerard and the Chautauqua Writer's Festival for encouraging me to begin writing. I am thankful for Joan Lee Hunter and her Beginning Writing Workshop as well. Both of these knowledgeable individuals know how to encourage a person to start writing. I found them both to be extremely helpful.

Ciao, for now. JB Zito

CPSIA information can be obtained at www.ICGtesting.com
Printed in the USA
LVOW042235011012

301047LV00003B/1/P

9 781466 929456